From Chaos to Creativity

From Chaos to Creativity

....

The Art and Practice of the EnergyWorks Method

KIM BELLISIMO, MA

Cover design by Frame25 Productions
Cover art by Africa Studio c/o Shutterstock.com
Print book interior design by Howie Severson

Turning Stone Press
8301 Broadway, Suite 219
San Antonio, TX 78209

Library of Congress Control Number
is available upon request.

ISBN 978-1-61852-132-3

10 9 8 7 6 5 4 3 2 1

Contents

Introduction

When people start on the path of self-discovery, they usually start with simple self-awareness exercises before moving on to mindfulness and meditation. But there is so much more to explore. In addition, when pursuing their dreams, many people do so almost entirely with their minds, which leaves no room for spontaneity and eliminates the possibility for anything new to manifest. To truly create the life you love, you must begin with your heart. Out beyond awareness and meditation, however, beyond the limited realm of the mind, is a Heart-centered path of co-creating from a place of wholeness and learning how to transform your own internal chaos into creativity so that you can live the life you love . . . and love the life you live. This path is EnergyWorks.

This book will take you on a journey to a place you didn't know existed. To get there, however, you have to start by accepting that you will not know where you're going. This acceptance will leave you open to receive something new. Throughout the book you will learn exercises that will help move you along this journey.

The tools in each of these chapters are meant to be used on a daily basis for two weeks. After the initial two weeks, you'll have conditioned your energy system to activate and integrate within your body and will be able to do the exercises in the moment. Don't dwell on thoughts about whether they're working or not; just do them. You will be connecting circuits so that your energy will flow.

I recently read a study about luck. Researchers discovered that the ability to see an opportunity that others couldn't see determined how lucky someone was. But most people don't know how to see from their Hearts, and how we see is how we create. So, in this book, you will learn how to see and create opportunities and also how you can create a new life by not knowing what it is you want to create. If we continue to see the world not as we know it but as we don't know it, then, like an innocent child, we will always be surprised.

As you move through the exercises, you'll experience how to be in the world in a new way. The point of the exercises is not about doing them right or perfectly. Doing the exercises is about getting you to be in the space around you—in the present moment—and creating a reality that, no matter what situation you're in, will bring in new and exciting things.

The material contained in this book is a combination of memoir, client case histories, and tools, along with a basic outline of my personal EnergyWorks philosophy. This book combines a story, viewpoint, and practice under one cover.

My own story, with its corresponding path to self-discovery, is interspersed in these chapters. It's a story of challenge, illness, and deprivation, and of inner vision and ultimate victory. Above all, it's a story of meaningful self-possession. It's also a story that's ongoing. The part that I'm sharing and the insights that accompany it are in and of themselves a work in progress.

The creation of this book represents, for me, the current culmination of a journey that has led from a childhood as a hoarder's daughter, with horrific health issues, a crippling lack of self-esteem, and a severe learning disability, to a thriving career as a transformational life coach with clients all over the world, and a woman with a healthy body, balanced life, and beautiful family.

It's a story about bulldozers and peacocks. And it all begins at the city dump.

1

Creating Out of Chaos

My dad used to take my brother and me to the city dump on weekends so that we could scavenge for treasures. I still vividly remember the smell, a combination of rotting garbage and sharp, tear-inducing toxic waste fumes from the refinery nearby.

Giant bulldozers moved huge mounds of trash around to create space. Amazingly, a group of wild peacocks lived off the refuse at the dump. Believe it or not, peacocks feed on poisons and metabolize them into what becomes the male peacocks' brilliant plumage.

From these early years onward, my life's work has been based on this joint metaphor of the bulldozer clearing space to allow more to come in and the peacock transforming toxic waste into something beautiful.

Since we didn't have money to go shopping, we'd load up the truck with tables, chairs, old toys, golf clubs, and umbrellas—anything we thought we could use. That is how we furnished our house. Once, we took home a TV that didn't work, but it was a nice piece of furniture. I sat in front of the TV, staring at the screen for hours, projecting my dreams and desires onto the dark, blank screen. Years later, I would come to understand that the dark, blank screen I stared at would become the canvasses for my new creations as I got older and learned how to project a picture.

Another place my dad loved to visit was the thrift store. This was where we got our clothes and gadgets. My dad collected everything, especially things that were broken and in need of repair. Although my dad could fix anything, he never did so and simply let all that stuff accumulate. Our home was reminiscent of the old TV show *Sanford and Son*, which was about an old man and his son living in a junkyard. Our yard was full of junk, and our house was full of clutter.

Everything dad started would end up unfinished. He once started to remodel our bathroom and I was so excited, but my excitement eventually wore off when I realized that he would never complete what he'd torn up. We didn't have a shower anymore, so for the next *eighteen years* we could only take a bath. The walls around the tub remained permanently exposed, a constant reminder that we didn't have money for repairs.

Dad was extremely talented, but his underlying desire was to have his own space. This desire was ironic since he couldn't even manage to create a small clearing in his own home. Yet, intuitively, on a subconscious level, he knew he needed space of some sort to be able to create. For example, my brother and I tried to create a garden in the backyard. We cleared the junk and the boards and planted seeds, but my father saw a clear space and parked his tar pot there, destroying our garden and any possibility of growth. Interestingly, as a young girl, I put a little vase with a pink flower in it on my dad's tar pot so that some growth and beauty, even the tiniest amount, would be reflected there.

My dad was a dreamer who had big ideas about what he could accomplish if he didn't have a family. He wanted to be an accomplished craftsman, he wanted to play more in his band, he wanted to become an artist, and he loved to cook and thought he could be a chef. He would carry books around with him to learn how to do all of this, but ironically, Dad couldn't read. And because he didn't know how to budget, my parents were always stressed and fighting about money.

Mom would get angry with Dad because he would buy things for himself (not for us) without telling her. He never let his lack of money get in the way because he was convinced that every shabby acquisition was a genuine antique. Dad felt controlled by Mom and accused her of blocking his dreams. These accusations made Mom feel unsafe, unsupported, and unstable.

Once, my brother and I found two large wooden dice at the dump. Mine had the number five on all sides and my brother's had the number two. These added up to the number seven, which my dad said was a lucky number. My dad's father had been a gambler. His gambling had gotten so out of control that he had to put my dad in foster care because he and my grandmother had split up and could no longer care for him. My dad moved between foster homes for the rest of his childhood, but he still kept in touch with Grandpa Victor. I sometimes think Dad kept broken things around because he identified with objects that had been discarded, just like he had been. To this day, I still am amazed that every house number of every house I have ever lived in adds up to the number seven.

From a young age, I remember constantly organizing Dad's stuff and trying to make it look beautiful. I would organize his shop, tools, and garage, and I would organize his truck. He had a used, junky truck that embarrassed me. The dashboard was his toolbox. He had tools and clipboards crammed there. There was even a plant growing on the dashboard. I could hardly find a place to sit. We were lucky we never got into an accident. I know now that my talent for organization has its roots in that truck.

Weekly, as my father brought piles of stuff home from the thrift store, my mom and I would sneak things out and return them. Our efforts often resulted in Dad doubling the money he spent because he'd actually wind up buying the same items over and over again. Mom and I started dropping things off at a thrift store in the next county because it was out of his driving range. Sometimes, he noticed what was missing and got angry. He still hasn't forgiven me for getting rid of a large aquarium that was sitting in the garage for over ten years.

After I went on to college and graduate school, I created the EnergyWorks method that has taken me all over the world. I've learned that people who are healers naturally focus on other people's needs. However, without an activated Heart-centered circuit, those who give continuously outside of themselves hardly ever receive anything in return.

Creating is about playing with ideas about what you want and what you don't want. By moving and playing, even in chaos, you will be able to learn how to create order out of chaos. You will be able to learn where your energy got stuck and stored or even hijacked so that you can access it to create something new. This process will involve using your awareness, directing your attention, moving toward your intention, and unifying all of these things in your Heart to create a brand-new life.

Along the way, you will learn how to play with, and discover things about, your energy and how to create with Mother Nature and Spirit. This co-creation will also involve keeping a journal and daily practices of clearing, creating space, and bringing in the unknown. The goal isn't about creating something specific; it's about moving energy around you and creating a vortex through which the creativity of the Universe can flow. You will learn how to occupy the eye of the storm, a place where you can experience peace, love, and support. This is the true safe space you need to be able to create and allow miracles to drop in.

Every day I work with people who want to create a new life for themselves. They want a healthy body, a happy relationship, financial abundance, and a new way to parent. I work with companies to help unify their organizations and to give their employees tools for achieving new goals. I help people realize their dreams.

Energy moves in a circuit, with an active and a passive side. When energy moves, change and flow occur. My practice is Heart-centered and is based on the premise that the ***Heart*** brings opposing sides into relationship, creating wholeness. My methodology therefore consists of teaching how to create from the whole, as opposed to being either stuck in the negative or swept along by the super-positive.

The mind can drive people's energy out of their bodies and out of their space. Often, people know exactly what they need to do to be healthy, but they continue to carry on destructive behavior. They continue in this way because their energy is divided between the negative and the positive. It is within this divided space that they remain stuck, without movement, stagnated. What shows up is depression, anxiety, fear, and paralysis.

My practice identifies what people want to create versus what they don't want to create and then brings the two sides into relationship through the Heart. The Heart pulls these opposites together, creating movement and flow. This energy, borne of wholeness, is what moves us toward our true Intentions and our true life's purpose.

Most people understand the concept of mindfulness, awareness, and meditation. However, to manifest the reality you want and to understand how creation happens, you must understand how your energy moves, changes, and transforms your life. I have dedicated decades to studying how this works and have created an easy-to-follow method of transformation, known as EnergyWorks. EnergyWorks has grown out of the scientific fact that everything in the Universe vibrates. Awareness is about observing. Meditation is about focusing. *EnergyWorks is about actively changing energy to change your life.* In this book there are meditations, exercises, and tools designed to help you change your vibration and your life.

When clients come to see me, they state their Intentions of what they want to create. Looking at them energetically, I can see the discrepancy between the vibration of what they want and the vibration that they are stuck in. My job is to get them to open their Hearts and create a circuit that in turn creates movement and flow, bringing them into relationship with what they want. When this happens, the negative within them shows up and must be released.

My clients often view this release of the negative as their lives falling apart, not realizing that the life they seek to change has been built on this false foundation, which is now collapsing into a new reality. I teach them how to use this release of negative energy as a source of power for creation.

When we're sitting on the beach, we don't think of the waves as being pushed out and pulled back—we simply tune into the flow. Similarly, in the process of creation, our energy moves out, and if we are Heart-centered, our energy comes back to complete a circuit, and it is this movement that allows us to change and grow.

As a little girl, I could see fields of energy. Some people had dark energy that made me anxious and afraid. Other people were filled with light and movement, and it seemed that miracles would happen around them. I was overtaken at times. I had learning disabilities and health issues, and I lived in isolation. But I became a student of my circumstances and always sought to move my life forward. It was my shift to a Heart-centered way of being that brought permanent positive change.

Now, for me, there is no greater joy or fulfillment than teaching people how to create, because together we can create something greater than we could ever create on our own, separate and apart. This is what I call the ***Greater Whole***, and it is for this purpose that I present this book.

Why do some people move from desperate beginnings to a happy, healthy life, while other people from advantageous backgrounds become helplessly stuck and unhappy? Why do some people seem to pursue their goals effortlessly and achieve them, while other people work ceaselessly and seem to get nowhere? This book is about taking what we're given and putting it to work. It's about dealing with the residual effects of events in our lives over which we have no control, but which we can take mastery of and transform. Finally—and I believe this is the book's most important lesson—it's about how to be the creator of your own life's story.

Simply by reading this book, you will start to activate your life in ways you never thought possible. As a whole, the book is designed to be an ongoing, constantly expanding exercise and guide. It's interesting to me that I'm writing all of this and learning from it in the process. I had never focused on my own story until the process of creating this book started to unfold. I've come to realize, as the book has progressed, that my life story is the basis for my work, and that only through a complete understanding of my own backstory can I free myself and redirect my energy in a way that will continue to transform my life.

Recently, I decided to free myself of my horizontal attachments. I used to give everything away, without receiving anything in return. But I learned (thanks to the athletes in my family) that the greatest sports teams are composed of players who have complete confidence in themselves and their teammates. They play an unselfish game, passing the ball to the teammate in the best position to advance, and they do so with the assurance that their teammates will do the same for them in return. In the simplest terms, the ball goes out and the ball comes back, and everyone in the long run thrives.

To completely transform my life, I committed to a vertical path. I had to establish myself as a priority and concentrate on choosing my own playing field. I had to give up on the notion that any person with whom I shared my energy would automatically send it back, and I had to commit to living my own life story.

To be truly effective as healers and humans on our own journeys, we must remain focused on our own playing field and create a reality that other people are invited to join.

By focusing on the steps outlined in this book, I stopped giving it all away. My life began to change the moment I moved my awareness to my Heart. Instead of using my energy to help others create, I moved my attention to my inner self. My profession is one of helping and healing, but one in which there is an exchange and an agreement, as opposed to expending energy without a flow of return. I invite you into that flow.

ENERGYWORKS METHOD

1. ***Identify it.*** Write down and identify a Picture in which your energy is stuck. When energy gets stuck at a certain moment in time, I call that a *Picture*. A Picture is like a momentary snapshot that provides insight into a larger story with a beginning, a middle, and an end, but one that keeps repeating itself, over and over again. This would be like visiting an art museum and going through the same gallery of pictures repeatedly. Over time, such Pictures accumulate. You store them. You continue to use them, and you continue to be stuck in the same old Pictures or moments in time, playing them out again and again. There is a saying that doing the same thing over and over again while expecting a different result is a form of insanity.

   Describe the setting. What blockages begin to appear? Remember, you are just watching a movie, instead of being in the movie. Don't get caught up in the drama. Describe the incident in detail from the beginning to the end, concluding this exercise by writing: "*I'm here right now.*" Now you have the freedom to change the storyline of your life, from moment to moment. As you progress through the Pictures that make up the story of your life, be aware of your thoughts and feelings. Your response creates your reality. Did you notice yourself shutting down, disconnecting, or feeling as if you ceased to exist at all? Many times, when we were younger, our feelings were hurt, and it only takes one incident for us to determine that we are not good enough, that we are stupid, or that we're not seen. Based on the thoughts, images, and Pictures in your journal, what responses did you have that might be distorted? Keep repeating this exercise until you are able to do so from a totally neutral point of view.

2. ***Move it.*** As you journal, notice if you become stuck in an emotion. Identify your feelings as you move through your storyline. Do you feel sad, shut down, or angry? As you move through the Pictures, you are collecting the energy that got stuck and stored and are bringing it into the present moment so that you can access it. By moving through the Pictures again and again, you will create space and find freedom.

3. ***Use it.*** Use the energy you have brought into the now. Use it to change the beginning, middle, and ending of your storyline. The more you can create new Pictures, the more you are freeing your creativity so that you won't get stuck creating the same old reality.

2

Use the Fuel of the Backspace to Create the Life You Want

When I was in my twenties, I received food stamps. My mother was unemployed, and we sat in my car together, trying to figure out how to make money. We quickly realized that we were both good at organizing, a skill we'd acquired from having to continuously organize my father's hoarded belongings. Based on our conversation that day, Mom and I knew that we could go into any home, office, or garage and create order out of chaos. So, together, we started the first organizing company that I'm aware of. We called our business Timesavers and our slogan was "We organize your time and life."

We began by posting simple flyers around town. When that didn't work, we made sandwich boards and walked around upscale Mill Valley, California, handing out our flyers. Although no one quite understood the concept of hiring an organizer (because it had never been done before), we certainly caught the attention of several onlookers.

Eventually, we began to get clients, and soon, feature stories were being written about us in local papers. We even received national publicity, in both *Woman's Day* and *Worth* magazines. The articles featured stories about clients whose belongings we organized and whose lives, for a period of time, we changed. What I came to learn, however, was that old patterns would resurface, and chaos would return. I realized that I would not only need to clear the clutter of actual objects in a physical space but would also have to clear negative thoughts that kept people trapped in specific patterns, habits, and routines.

All of my "training" with my father's hoarding came in handy, years before hoarding was a commonly known syndrome. My mother and I became specialists in our field. We'd get calls from social workers on behalf of people who were evicted from their homes, who could regain access only if the homes became habitable. Entering homes filled, quite literally, from floor to ceiling was like being at the city dump again. I thrived where others felt overwhelmed by the chaos in front of them.

My mom and I also moved people from one place to another. We would literally pack up all of their belongings, unpack them at the other end, and put their things away while, at the same time, organizing them. We also worked for hundreds of senior citizens, downsizing them into homes that were often less than half the size of where they had been living, or into assisted living facilities that offered them a fraction of their old living space. These people had decades' worth of accumulated possessions, acquired during different phases of their lives. How do you part with a lifetime of memories? Thankfully, I knew what people needed and knew where things could go. One client's praise was especially memorable: "It was after *Timesavers* organized me that I finally realized I didn't need a therapist." While that client truly believed that she no longer needed a therapist, the truth was that organizing her physical space was not enough. *True, sustained change happens only on the energetic level.*

Through this work, I discovered that I loved helping people bring order out of chaos so that they could create something new in their lives. But more importantly, my work with hoarders made me recognize the patterns these people shared with my father. They became attached to objects in a similar way. They ran their energy into the objects until the objects became, in *their* minds, an extension of themselves.

These people felt safe, secure, stable, and supported by the objects around them because the objects wouldn't abandon them, and they could conjure a state of security and stability based on the objects' permanence.

One ninety-nine-year-old female client held a vase while I was unpacking and said, "Thank God this vase is still intact because it outlasted seven of my husbands. You can't count on people, but this object is like my best friend that won't leave or abandon me." In a very real sense, my clients' objects became their families. When things began to pile up, whether office papers or clothes or items in storage, knowing where to start to address the issue would throw them into a state of internal chaos and make them passive. I had been enlisted to organize their external chaos, but it became clear to me that nothing would be accomplished in the long run without teaching my clients to turn inward.

I discovered that by analyzing a person's external environment and organizational issues, I could gain insight into that person's inner life, specifically with regard to their current transitions. I could ascertain whether they were going through a career transition or a relationship issue, if they had an unrevealed addiction, or if they were undergoing family turmoil. I saw that people were running depression and anxiety into their objects. When I'd walk into the home of an alcoholic, even in their absence, I could feel their addiction as if it were vibrating out of the very objects in the room. It was clear to me that the outer world of my clients was a reflection of their inner chaos. I reasoned that if I could somehow work in reverse to help them access their inner world first, then the changes that they so desperately sought in their outer worlds would remain permanently.

To create a lasting solution to my client's issues, I needed to start by setting an energetic vibration of their goals and intentions directly into the objects in their home. This new vibration would affect the person positively in the long term. I call this process "setting space," and I teach it to my clients today so that they can match the vibrations that I have set in the objects as a way of supporting them in their environments. I soon learned that I could do this either in person or remotely. *My clients came to learn that changing their energy changed their lives.*

Bringing awareness and consciousness into a space became my real work as an organizer, something that my clients had never consciously acknowledged. Although I was still a hands-on organizer, I often found myself sitting with people and talking through the process. When someone picked up an object, there would be an attachment to it or an emotional connection. They would start to tell me a story about what the item meant to them and why they couldn't get rid of it. Some of the items were insignificant, but like any memorabilia, they reminded the clients of a time and space when they went somewhere or did something that seemed important or brought them joy or even pain. The objects represented moments in which their energy became stuck and stored, and my job was to walk my clients through a process of letting these things go and accessing the energy.

My process consisted of pulling their energy out of a given object (and the space and time to which it was connected and stuck) so that they were able to release their attachments and finally let them go, which meant that they would have more access to their own energy to create the lives they truly wanted.

I soon developed a process of witnessing the energy that passed between people and their objects. I saw objects as energy containers, energy that had its source in what I began to refer to as a person's Backspace.

My clients had transferred their energy to objects that were connected to previous experiences. Those objects not only became repositories for their often-misguided energy but also constantly reflected it back to them over time.

I saw that I was clearly dealing with people who were trapped in an ongoing cycle, or loop, of energy that they couldn't escape from. This energy accumulated into piles of objects, mountains of paperwork, and backed-up appointments, and the more my clients accumulated, the more stagnant their energy became. Getting them to let go of physical objects was the first step in getting them to confront their issues, but getting them to release the energy of those objects was what eventually moved their lives forward because it created space.

Through all of these encounters, I realized that my vocation needed to be centered on bringing awareness and consciousness back into my clients' physical space. Otherwise, they would remain unconscious and wouldn't have enough energy in their bodies to clear out their spaces.

As explained by the great physicist Albert Einstein, all objects vibrate at a certain frequency. I found that the easiest way to support my clients was to make changes in their physical space by clearing the stuck and stored energy of both my clients' objects and their physical space. Then I set new vibrations of the objects and the physical spaces in which my clients lived and worked. Finally, I contained the energy of the physical spaces. This process created a safe, secure, stable, and supportive environment in which their energy would return to them, thus setting the stage for them to grow.

For example, a client contacted me because her daughter had symptoms of autism that had worsened to the point where her daughter could barely speak. While on the phone with my client, I scanned the physical environment, her daughter's energy field, and the family's genetic line. I could see an object in her daughter's room that had a frequency anchored in her daughter's throat. I asked my client if she had an object in her daughter's room that had belonged to someone who had passed away. My client told me that her daughter was sleeping with a doll that had once belonged to her late grandmother. I suggested my client remove the doll, and overnight, there was a huge energetic shift. Her daughter began talking again.

Another client called and told me that her two children were getting into all sorts of accidents and that she and her husband were fighting all the time. I asked her what, if any, new objects she had recently brought into her home. She told me that she had received some jewelry from her mother-in-law, who was an abusive alcoholic, and the frequency of her behaviors, I discovered, was causing the aforementioned chaos.

I can clear objects, but sometimes our ancestors' or other people's energy becomes so attached to these objects that their energy gets fragmented and stuck to them, not unlike, believe it or not, the Horcruxes in the *Harry Potter* book series. Our ancestors can't fully move on if they have passed away, or, if they are alive, their energy remains fragmented and stuck.

An object will start to run a frequency through a space and will start to collapse the reality that exists to be able to match that frequency, causing chaos. Those who live in that environment must match that frequency, which is why their lives start to fall apart.

Another client, who had been diagnosed with colon cancer, came to see me. I could see that the cancer vibrated through the female line on her dad's side of the family. My client had been fine until she went to live at a family home that had previously been rented out and that had been partially furnished with her late paternal grandmother's possessions. When my client moved in, her health began to rapidly decline.

The frequency that objects contain can vibrate so strongly that a person's energy field will collapse into the reality of the previous owner of the objects if that person does not have a strong enough energy field.

Most people live with objects from families, friends, or consignment and thrift stores. If a loving and supportive person is the original source of an object, it can have a positive effect. But you must be aware of your physical space and whether the objects in that space support you.

In this chapter you will learn how to clear objects and set the objects and vibrations in your environment so that they are safe, secure, stable, and supportive. If we accumulate too many objects in our environment and there isn't enough space for energy to move, energy becomes sticky and slow. Then we end up matching the vibrations of those objects, and it becomes hard to move our energy and use our energy to create, because to create something new, we need space. For example, a person may want to get up and go to the gym but finds that they cannot because they don't have enough energy in their body due to the objects in their environment. The frequency of objects is slow compared to ours, so if you are surrounded by lots of things, you won't use your energy, and if you don't use it and move it, energy becomes stuck and stored. If you don't have enough energy to create change in your physical environment, you have to start moving your energy and, in turn, your body. That is the way to start to create change in your life.

Most of us have accumulated a lifetime of experiences and interactions during which our energy was trapped in particular Pictures that became stuck and stored. When you don't have access to the energy and information in these Pictures, a part of you becomes frozen and movement ceases. This is when creativity also ceases to exist.

The *Backspace* is like a storage shed where you place your old memories, holding onto ideas because you think you will need them in the future. But if you don't move your energy, it becomes stuck, stored, and inaccessible. *What is in your Backspace? Any moment in time when you experienced pain, trauma, fear, and anxiety that caused your energy to split from your body, causing you to stop existing in that moment.*

Did you ever get picked on or bullied? Was one of your parents a narcissist who had to make every situation about him or her so that you were never seen or felt to exist? Were you in an abusive situation, or did you buy into someone's opinion that you were ugly or stupid? Did someone make a comment about how overweight you were or how you weren't good at sports or that you were clumsy?

These are all Pictures that people project onto you. These Pictures become a part of your programming that you live and create by. When three or more Pictures are projected onto you at a young age, you believe them to be true, and you start accepting them as your own. A part of your energy becomes trapped in these Pictures, which then start to define you. The Pictures act like agreements between you and the people who projected them onto you, preventing you from creating what you want.

Your Backspace also becomes a place for others to dump their own pain. You take on *their* Pictures to try to heal *them*, get *them* unstuck, and move *their* energy. But when you do this, you take on *their* information, *their* energy, and *their* pain and, as a result, you become stuck in *their* Pictures. *Have you ever had a friend call you and tell you how depressed they were and you spent an hour listening to someone else's story, offering advice, trying to fix the situation, only to hang up and realize that now, suddenly, you are depressed?*

You become another person's dumping ground because you want to help them and heal them, but in doing so, you open yourself up to being overtaken. The more energy you take on, the less you are able to move. You may experience this as gaining weight, developing a health issue or addiction, or becoming unmotivated to move toward your goals.

Not only do you become programmed by others who project their Pictures onto you, but you also project Pictures onto yourself, reinforcing the story that isn't true but that you believe to be true. Maybe, as a child, you were not a strong student or athlete or were told that you were too sensitive or that your thoughts and feelings did not matter.

The moment we formulate an opinion of ourselves, whether based on our own assumptions or the assumptions of others, we trap our energy.

Worse, once you become resigned to a negative opinion projected onto you by another person, you give up hope and "get into agreement" with this false reality that keeps you isolated and in despair, full of self-doubt and self-loathing. And no matter what you do, you are unable to move beyond it, so you continue to play it out in your life. That Picture then becomes the self-sabotaging block in the road that prevents you from moving forward.

The truth is that we are not our Pictures, and we have the ability to change and transform our Pictures, creating a new life story.

The Backspace is an accumulation of the energy that's stuck and stored in Pictures. It keeps us from moving forward in our lives. Our minds may be able to set Intentions, but our bodies are unable to move. So, to create anything, we must access that energy to use it and move it. By having this awareness, we have the ability to use it as the fuel to move forward in a new Picture.

The Backspace is important because it shows you where you've been stuck in a false Picture. It's a place where you can observe and recreate the distorted Pictures that have been binding you so that you can use them to catapult you out into your new reality.

Most people think that being negative or feeling sad is an undesirable state to be in.

But if we can understand what the feelings and observations of the negative events that occurred in our life are really trying to show us, then we can embrace them and resolve the issues they represent, thanking them for what we learned from them and the strength we gained from being able to resolve them.

This feedback counteracts denial and distortion and leads to truth and forward movement. The purpose of the Backspace, therefore, is to communicate with us, by showing us the place where our energy has become stuck and to allow us to set it free.

The Backspace will continue to create situations that will play out certain energetic patterns until you have mastered the lesson you came here to learn and have freed your energy from that particular Picture so that you can move on.

For example, a client of mine grew up with a narcissistic mother, who trained my client to keep her attention on her mother's needs and wants. As a result, my client never learned to focus on herself. She went to college and immediately fell head over heels for a handsome, charismatic narcissist, who demanded all of my client's attention and controlled her just as her mother had done. She married him and started to disappear. She no longer knew who she was. The abuse and control became worse, yet she stayed in the Picture, believing that she had to rescue this man and heal him, until she became so sick that she had to leave, despite being financially cut off, forcing her to move in with a narcissistic relative, repeating, once again, many of the patterns she had lived through with her mother and husband. Years later, after working with me and her Backspace, she realized that she was done with this Picture and moved forward into her new reality. This is the classic Cinderella story. My client believed that she would be safe if she continued to give to the wants and needs of the threat (that is, the narcissists who controlled her, whom she mistakenly believed would keep her safe). She broke the spell by turning her attention inward so that she could start creating a new life for herself.

If we continue to remain stuck in the Pictures of our past, they will eventually show us where we left the door open for others to run their requests, demands, anger, energy, or aggression through us.

You may feel bullied, threatened, or experience real fear in your space so that you continue doing what others want you to do. The Backspace even has the ability to move your energy through other people to get *them* to play out painful situations with you, enforcing your belief that your pain is real. This is where you have to take responsibility for what your energy is doing and creating.

When you experience abuse of any kind, your energy leaves your body. You may choose to look at and analyze a stored Picture and talk about it or talk around it, but to be truly free of it, you must return to the moment and watch it like a movie. Doing this gives you access to the Picture so that you can move it and use it to create a new Picture that contains new, updated information to change the way you create.

The field of epigenetics, which deals with environmental and situational trauma, has demonstrated that past trauma is stored in our bodies' cells and can be passed down to offspring. As a result, people come into the world with issues and anxieties that they are unable to resolve because they think those problems are theirs, but in fact they have inherited them. It is up to them to use that energy to transform their future, as well as their past. When they do this, even the lives of their family members will begin to transform.

The information and exercises in this chapter will give you the tools to begin to clear your stuck and stored

Pictures. As you start to do this, you may feel as though you have an insurmountable pile of junk to discard. But take Heart. Like the bulldozer at the city dump, if you clear some space for something new to come through, your energy will start to move and flow.

Client Story

A client named Sandy initially came to me because she had health issues. She was in a job in which both her coworkers and bosses were dismissive, and she didn't feel appreciated. She began drinking a glass of wine nightly to relax, as a way to cope with her anxiety and fear. Her relationship with her body was anxiety-producing because her energy was always outside of her body, and she often found herself daydreaming about different Pictures of her past and future, including being fired and her coworkers talking behind her back.

We started to look at places in her life where her energy had disconnected from the present moment, that is, where she had lost her relationship with her body and had thereby become ungrounded, and where, consequently, her energy had become frozen in time. The common theme of her daydreams had to do with health issues and fears about herself and her family members. For example, Sandy always feared that something terrible was going to happen to her daughter when her daughter went out with friends. Sandy's Backspace kept repeating the same Pictures over and over again—something was going to happen to her or the people she loved—and these Pictures continued to reinforce her fear and anxiety.

After reviewing these Pictures with Sandy, I could see that most of her energy was connected to her birth. Once we reviewed the circumstances surrounding her birth, I could see a clear Picture connecting her to her anxiety and fear. That Picture involved Sandy's mother. Prior to conceiving Sandy, Sandy's mother had given birth to a child who died three days later. Sandy's mother's energy had become stuck and stored in that traumatic moment, and that Picture kept replaying in her Backspace so that all of her future offspring were affected.

Seven months into her pregnancy with Sandy, in September, Sandy's mother started hemorrhaging and almost lost Sandy. It was yet another traumatic moment that reinforced Sandy's mother's core Picture that the world was not a safe space and that something bad would happen to her children. (For example, six months later, an infant Sandy had a choking incident and was rushed to the hospital, barely surviving.)

Over the years, Sandy routinely experienced depression every September, a pattern that culminated in her thirties, when she attempted to take her own life. She never put the near-death incident in her mother's womb, just before birth, together with her chronic and chronological bouts of anxiety and deep depression. Only when we went back through her Pictures to discover the source of her particular pain were we able to free her energy and allow it to be accessed in present time.

In our sessions together, Sandy and I learned that she had reached conclusions about her life based on distorted Pictures of herself and how terrifying it was to be alive. But these distorted Pictures had been passed down to her by her mother. Sandy was then able to bring herself back into those horrifying (at the time) moments and move herself through them. She became the creator of her own reality by creating new Pictures of how the world would support her. Together, we created new Pictures of her birth, and instead of being born into a world full of fear and anxiety, Sandy saw herself being born into a safe and supportive one.

Sandy is in her sixties now and for the past three years has been studying homeopathy. She is excelling in her studies and has committed to moving her energy in her body because it has transformed her health and supports her homeopathic philosophy. Sandy had always dreamed of doing what she loved but never had the energy to pursue the right career because she was always so fatigued. Now she has a newfound purpose and passion for helping people come back into their bodies, because when a person is fully in the body, that person is healthy, vibrant, and thriving. Moreover, Sandy's work on herself has also positively affected her own daughter.

By releasing and clearing the stored energy of those old Pictures, Sandy was free to move her energy and her life forward in a new and fulfilling way.

ENERGYWORKS METHOD
Clearing Stored Energy in Yourself, Your Environment, and Your Objects

1. ***Identify and access the energy.*** Take a visual inventory of one item or area in your home (or office) or an area in your life where you want to create change. Notice if there are areas you have not touched that feel like dead weight. Notice if you want to clean up your physical space but don't have the energy to get up off the couch and do it. Notice if you start thinking about an area in your life but become overwhelmed and fatigued. If you are looking at your physical space, notice where you feel your energy

is stuck. This may be the place where you have a pile of papers stacked up or a cluttered closet. If you leave your objects sitting without accessing them (moving them and using them for their intended purposes), the energy in your home or space will start to become sticky or heavy. Be aware of any thoughts that start rising to the surface. Do you want to give up? Are you becoming overwhelmed? Identify your feelings. Do you feel sad or angry? Are you experiencing bodily sensations? Does your stomach hurt? You are looking at an area of your life that isn't working because energy is stuck and stored. You are simply identifying what isn't working. Keep going. Just by identifying it, you can start to access the stored energy and do something with it.

2. ***Release the energy and let go.*** Your energy not only gets stuck in Pictures or experiences in your body but also gets stuck in objects, jewelry, photographs, furniture, and clothing—all of the things people, including ourselves and our ancestors, have owned. If a particular object belonged to someone else, then that person's energy (which may include depression, addiction, fear, anxiety, or even an unknown energy) is vibrating in it and therefore in your space, impacting your life, so you need to bring consciousness to the object to set it free.

    To release the energy of old Pictures or the stuck energy of objects, connect your Heart to the Picture or object (while holding, touching, or imagining it) with your left hand, while saying to the energy in the object, "Release and let go." When you clear an object that has been passed down from your genetic line, not only do you become unstuck, but you also create movement, space, and freedom for yourself and your ancestors. Most importantly, when it comes to Pictures, you won't play out that same reality again and again.

3. ***Set a new vibration.*** To either create "new" Pictures or set objects with a "new" vibration, imagine a new Picture, or hold or touch an object with your right hand, while saying, "Renew." If you are setting an object, focus on an object in the environment and just observe it. Set a vibration, like joy, into that object and let yourself match that frequency. Move your breath to that object and back into your Heart, breathing in joy and exhaling any negative energy. Focusing on an object will anchor your energy in the moment so that your energy won't abandon your space. For example, you connect your Heart to the object and tune into the vibration you want to be in, such as peace, love, or enthusiasm. You can even set a color that you like. While tuning into your Heart, state your Intention; for example, "I have an amazing job, where I am seen and recognized and compensated beyond my wildest dreams!" Then, imagine the energy emanating out of your Heart, into the object, then out into your environment, like a vibrating gong, sending sound waves of energy of how you are "being" in this present moment.
   By doing this, your environment will support your state of being, even if you don't believe it. Your environment will start to match the new energy. For example, I have set the energy of the garage in my house at a vibration of working out and exercising. Now, no matter who walks into my garage, even if they don't work out, they start exercising!

Journaling

This five- to ten-minute exercise will help you observe and witness where your energy is stored and stuck. You will be able to move through your Pictures, just like looking through a photo album, so that you won't have to recreate that reality in your life again and again. Sometimes even identifying Pictures will stop them from playing out. Moving through the beginning, middle, and ending of a story made up of a lot of Pictures will allow you to move your energy out of those Pictures and reclaim your energy in the present time so that you can then create a new story in which you feel safe, secure, stable, and supported. When creating the unknown, I say, "It's not in the how, it's in the now." By bringing our energy into the now, we prevent ourselves from becoming stuck in a particular storyline. When we are not attached to an outcome, we have the creative freedom to play and create new stories.

Now imagine your journal (either online or on paper) like a movie screen. See the computer screen or paper and notice the space between you and them. Maintain your distance by separating yourself from actually playing a part in the story you are writing. This way, you will maintain objectivity. Taking this step is important so that you don't get sucked back into creating the same old reality. When you can observe a scene that has happened to you without moving into it, you are no longer attached to it, and your energy will no longer get stuck or stored. Then you can change it. The observer creates the reality.

You must first discover what viewpoint you are stuck in. Look at your Picture. As you view the Picture's particular storyline again and again by writing it down, make sure to describe the setting of each scene. The more details you can recall, the more your information and energy will return to you. Keep writing the scene again and again until you have completed the beginning, middle, and ending and are no longer stuck. You will notice you are no longer emotionally charged and have the freedom to move out of that Picture and create a new Picture. If we don't pay attention to these Pictures, our Backspace will create more problems with our health, home, work, and relationships until we address them.

3

Awareness of What's in Your Space

I developed back trouble when I was very young. My dad had struggled with back pain for most of his life, and I remember him being in traction and unable to move for months at a time. I ended up with the same back issue. It was centered in my lower spine, an area of the body that I later learned metaphysically correlates with financial instability.

I had been teaching aerobics since I was fifteen, and now, at the age of twenty-five, my body started to fall apart. My joints were aching, and I could hardly lift my arms. My lower back was in so much pain that I could barely walk. An orthopedic surgeon diagnosed bursitis in both shoulders, a narrowing disc, and two herniated discs. I was constantly fatigued. I was depressed because I couldn't exercise and generate the necessary endorphins to keep my brain healthy and my spirits up. I ended up living on food stamps while I searched for medical answers.

Chronic fatigue was not yet widely known. My orthopedist mentioned that he was going to a nearby restaurant that evening to hear a lecture about fibromyalgia. I soon began hearing different doctors talk about the symptoms of fibromyalgia, and I felt tremendous relief because those symptoms corresponded to all of the symptoms I was experiencing. Then blood tests revealed I also had a thyroid disorder, which explained my need for constant sleep.

A naturopath discovered parasites in my system that were causing at least part of my fibromyalgia. I was relieved to have identified what was wrong with me, but no subsequent treatments seemed to help. I was given steroid injections for the bursitis, which only made the bursitis worse. And then my stomach began to hurt. Every day I suffered intense stomach cramps; everything I ate appeared to bring them on.

I eventually took medication to treat the parasites, which seemed to help, and my thyroid started to function more normally. But my life, in the wake of all of these health issues, was at a standstill. Since I no longer had a job, I house-sat.

At one point I rented a room from a recovered alcoholic, who suffered extreme fear and anxiety. This is when my health really declined. My energy would disappear when I spent time with other people, and I felt as if they were overtaking me. I was also diagnosed with Lyme disease.

I was so desperate and debilitated that I couldn't move. The more I drifted away from my body, the harder it was to return, and no matter what I did, I couldn't seem to find my way back. I was searching for answers outside of myself, but everyone else seemed just as unconscious as I was.

Awareness is our ability to observe the space around us and our energy within that space so that we don't disappear. When our energy leaves our space, it is like the tide going out. That is when we lose our life's force and become sick. The first step toward transforming my life was to become aware of what my energy was doing.

Awareness entails observing something without having an opinion about it, without trying to change it, and without having a conversation with it.

I had been active my whole life, pushing myself, taking action, and getting things done, so now I was at the point where I could not move. I was forced to just *be* in my sickness. The first step in my recovery was being aware of how I felt, listening to my body, and tuning into what it was telling me.

I was forced to stop and be present in the space around me. I realized that most of the actions that I had taken were in response to the chaotic energy of the space that I had occupied. I thought that if I could just keep changing my external world, like moving furniture from place to place in my home, somehow my life would change.

At this point, I couldn't move anything (myself or my furniture), and I had to face the energy and information moving in my space. Without resistance on my part, I became aware of a more subtle energy, one that you can't see with the eyes, but that on a very deep level can transform a person's space. I was forced to remain still yet could observe how everything around me was vibrating: my desk, the objects around me, things that would normally seem stagnant were vibrating. I began to focus on this same vibration within me.

Movement on the subtle level was my path to freedom.

But my path to freedom took some time, and I was heartbroken because I felt that I had no future. My heart was in so much pain that all I could do was focus on it. I focused on my heart beating; I felt like an infant listening to my mother's heartbeat. The sound of my heart and its rhythm relaxed my breath, and this anchored me into my body. I put my hand on my heart and started to focus on my breath while being aware of my heartbeat. I started to move my breath into the places where I felt pain and then back into my heart.

After repeating this process several times, I began to feel space in those places that were closed off. This circuit was the fundamental movement from my heart, through my pain, and back into my heart; this is what anchored my energy into my space.

I committed myself to repeating this process every day, first for five minutes and, eventually, twenty. Within a month, I began to transform. I had more awareness of what my body needed and wanted. This is when I started to be in relationship with my body instead of overriding it by always doing, doing, doing—sometimes driving it to extremes. I started to thrive as my energy slowly returned. Simply focusing on my pain and connecting my heart's energy to it brought me back into relationship with my body, my energy, and my space. It was this relationship that brought me back to life.

Opening to the Wisdom of your Heart allows you to own and occupy your space so that you can be aware of the energy and information that is around you. This awareness enables you to discern your energy from someone else's and to be aware of what your energy is doing. If you don't own and occupy your space with your own energy, other people will overtake you, and you will get programmed out of what *YOU* want to create with *YOUR* energy. As a result, you end up being used energetically by other people to achieve their goals. When you own your own energy in your own space, you have radiant health and wellness. Awareness, then, is knowledge of where your energy resides. Just having this awareness can shift everything for you.

Client Story

My client Lily, a woman in her early thirties, suffers from Lyme disease, which results in a host of symptoms including physical fatigue, confusion, and depression. Lily's mother also had a history of chronic illness, and she used Lily as a dumping ground for all of her fears and anxieties. When Lily reacted against this behavior, her mother's overt, almost oppressive, nature would make Lily feel guilty. This was a setup for Lily's own health issues and a template for her being overtaken by other people.

Lily's partner of fifteen years was accustomed to flying off the handle and lambasting her, constantly threatening to leave the relationship but never carrying through. Lily disliked her job and was treated with both anger and disrespect by her bosses and coworkers. As a result, she developed a mousy personality, barely spoke above a whisper, and was completely unable to assert herself. The boundaries between her energy and that of others were nonexistent. Even her health-care providers treated her angrily, resulting in her leaving her treatment sessions feeling run over, needing days to recover.

When Lily came to me and I looked at her energy field, I saw that only about 5 percent of her own energy was occupying her space. I could see that she was actually strong, intuitive, and an empath by nature, but she was taking on other people's issues in a misguided role as healer and, consequently, being completely overtaken by them. She mistook the thoughts and feelings of those who surrounded her as her own and began to question her sanity.

I began by helping Lily become aware of the energy in her space and how it could disappear in a moment, leaving her vulnerable to attack. We implemented steps to find and use her awareness so that she could navigate being around people in a safe and healthy way.

The first thing that shifted for Lily was her relationship with her partner. Next, by being committed to retaining her energy (instead of vacating her space out of fear), Lily also gained new respect at work. Finally, her mother, after so many years, no longer had permission to dump her issues onto Lily, and their relationship transformed as well.

Lily's health continues to improve. Her personality has become vibrant, and she's moving forward with joy in her life. Her Backspace is clearing the stored, distorted Pictures that allowed other people to dump their energy into her space. Because she has established boundaries that were never there before, letting her own energy fill her space, these old Pictures are now being used as fuel to propel her forward. The new Pictures that are replacing the old ones are those of health, vibrancy, and clear boundaries.

Lily can now more easily identify the energy vampires who overtake her space. She values relationships above all else, and sometimes it's hard for her to discern those who are supportive, kind, and collaborative. However, she has learned that even if someone is kind and caring initially, if they pull upon her energy, ignore her, or cut her off, these are all signs that she is being scammed out of her energy. People feed on the energy of others because it is what they need to create with; they specifically seek out people who are givers and those who value relationships. Lily became aware of this type of energy, and this awareness was the key to her restored health. It took about a year for Lily to unwind all of the destructive relationships she was in, for fear of being alone. The cost of getting sick wasn't worth it. Now Lily has a supportive community around her.

ENERGYWORKS METHOD
Clearing, Creating, and Receiving the Unknown

1. ***Be aware of the Diamond of the Heart.*** Place your hands over your heart. Say, "I open to the Wisdom of my Heart." Open your hands so the index fingers and thumbs are touching. This creates a portal in the shape of a Diamond.

2. ***Bring awareness to your space and then draw or write what you notice on paper.*** Be aware of the space around you. You can imagine your space as a bubble-like container that is filled with energy and information. Be aware of the energy and information occupying your space. Be aware of any thoughts, feelings, and sensations in your body. Spend five minutes being aware of what energy and information are in your space, without trying to change them. Is what you're looking at YOUR energy? Or is it someone else's? Ask your awareness to shine a light on it and make it known.

3. ***Be aware of your breath.*** Be aware of your breath. Inhale, as your breath moves to the top of the circle. Where there's a space, hold your breath and gaze at the space in between. That's the miracle space of your dreams. As you exhale, follow the line down to the bottom of the circle. Hold your breath and gaze at the empty space in between. Repeat the cycle and the breath in the circuit. As you inhale, be aware of your breath filling up your body with your vital energy. As you exhale, be aware of your breath releasing other people's energy or information out of your space.

4. ***Be aware of any blocks.*** As you're drawing or writing what shows up for you, notice if there are any blocks and, if so, where they are in your body or your space. Be aware of your heart and your breath. Be aware of where you feel pain in the body or where you feel blocked. Are there areas you have forgotten? Or places in the body that are closed off? Any doors you have closed because of past wounds? Put one hand on your heart and the other hand on the pain, or where you feel blocked or stuck. If you can't put your hand there, just set that intention. From your heart, connect your breath to the block, or pain, in the body and circulate it back to the heart. Be aware of your heart, be aware of the pain, and be aware of the breath connecting them in a circuit. Be aware of the heart's energy moving to the block and the block moving into the heart. Be aware if the two areas are connected and if there is a circuit. Just keep breathing and be aware of this relationship. By asking the

Wisdom of your Heart to open, you are opening a portal to welcome your energy back into your heart. This is how you can experience the feeling of being whole and how you bring the fragmented parts of yourself back together.

5. ***Ask your awareness to shine a light on any areas that are blocked.*** Be with this energy, instead of trying to fix it. What are you feeling? Don't hide or run from your feelings. Feel your feelings and be with them.

6. ***Notice what arrives in your awareness (thoughts, memories, experiences) over the next couple of days.*** This work is very deep, and you may not always be conscious of what blocks you may have in the moment. Some deep blocks may float to the surface. You are setting an intention, and it may take twenty-four to forty-eight or more hours for the truth to reveal itself. Be patient. When the blocks surface, in the form of patterns or even other people's behaviors, simply notice them and say, "Hello, it's time to let you go." Being aware of what you want to let go of, instead of what you want to bring in, will bring you into balance. *We are part of a society that is focused on consuming instead of letting go, and this can lead to constipation—physically, emotionally, and energetically*. Open up the flow to say, "Hello." Then let it go. This will result in the necessary space in your life to create something new.

Journaling

What do you notice in your space? Ask your awareness to shine its light on what it wants you to observe. Then notice what you begin to think about. Journal about it. By looking at the energy and information in your space, your energy will start to shift. Write for five to ten minutes about what is coming up for you. These exercises are an opportunity to practice awareness of what's in your space without judgment. When you have a judgment or reaction about what you see, what you're seeing will start to distort and shift. This is an important lesson about creating because you need to interact with your true energy to create something solid. Say you're in a relationship with someone and you don't accept them the way they are. They will begin to hide who they are to avoid conflict. You think you're creating with a certain reality, but you're not. You're engaging with a false reality. As a result, what you create together is not real and won't last. For this journaling exercise, you can either write about this experience or draw it. For example, on a piece of paper, you can draw a stick figure with a bubble around it. As you sit in your awareness, mark with colored pencils the areas of your body or your space where you feel energy and what you think, feel, or see there. Don't judge any of it as good or bad. Just create a drawing or write down what you are aware of in your space.

4

Attention

When I was in second grade, it became apparent that I had a severe learning disability, combined with an attention deficit that caused me to speak in fragmented sentences. The teacher, unaware of my real difficulties and blaming my classwork problems on lax attention, reacted by screaming at me violently, causing me to wind up in tears while the other kids laughed. I simply couldn't make a connection between written words and the thoughts they represented, and I resigned myself to failure where learning was concerned. This incident shattered my self-esteem. All of my energy left my body, and the circumstances of being attacked created a stored Picture in my Backspace that played out over the years. I responded by dissociating, which ultimately creates health problems.

This circumstance was something my father could identify with because he, too, had a learning disability and attention deficit disorder and only finished sixth grade. He would start projects but finish only about 60 percent of each one; then he would get kicked out of his space. Because over time he had so many of these uncompleted projects under his belt, so to speak, his energy became so disbursed that he couldn't collect up enough energy to complete other projects in his life, and for each project he began, he finished less and less. This inability to complete projects reinforced his low self-esteem and made him feel like a failure. Again, you can only create with the amount of energy you have in your space. So, you must always know where your energy is located (where it got stuck and stored) and call it back so that you can create in the present time.

My dad's aunt, my Great Aunt Lillian, had been orphaned but graduated school with a nursing degree. She was a specialist in hypnotherapy and was, in fact, one of the first people who taught hypnotherapy to medical practitioners. My father asked her to work with me, and at the age of eight, I was taught self-hypnosis. In my case, it was a process designed to subconsciously provide me with tools that would enhance my capacity for learning. This is what got me through high school with a "C" average.

Years later, in community college, I discovered that to find my energy and retrieve it from where it had gotten stuck, I had to go back in time to second grade. I entered a special on-campus program, was officially tested for learning disabilities, and was diagnosed with dyslexia and ADHD. Just being aware of my diagnoses gave me the energy I needed to continue my educational pursuits and to clear my Backspace.

My Aunt Lillian was extremely intuitive. Like ours, her house was filled with clutter and junk, but to my young eyes, her stuff was intriguing. She had crystals, fairies, and magic wands. She also loved science and read extensively. I was in tenth grade before I finally learned to read. I was also very shy and had a hard time finding my voice or even carrying on a simple conversation. Most people couldn't follow my train of thought because my thoughts were so scattered and didn't follow a sequential order. So, Lillian and I created affirmation cards that I would read three times a day, after putting myself in a light trance. While reading the cards, I was supposed to focus on my emotional response to achieving the specific goal on the card.

I remember comparing my own life and Aunt Lillian's when things became difficult for me. Aunt Lillian had an ongoing inability to create income and achieve financial success, and I wondered how hypnosis, based on her own example, could possibly be working. I asked her that question and she was offended, but I loved going to her house because it seemed magical. She had a way of pointing out unlimited possibilities and convincing me that I could create anything.

This experience with self-hypnosis was my first introduction to the subconscious and my first experience with the process of trying to transform my life. However, I found that though the tools were helpful, my learning disability persisted. What I did discover was my intuition. This entailed not only an ability to "see" the energy of other people but also a tendency to absorb and reflect it. Being sensitive on that level can make for a difficult life. It's like tuning into a frequency that your body starts to match. At the time, it seemed to me that when people had unpleasant thoughts, I could somehow feel them. I was sad and cried a lot because I could feel that energy come into my body, and it felt like a curse. The intuitive resources that had manifested in my early youth were brought out. The innate ability to read someone's energy freed me to look at the world in a different way, and people became my books.

There's a great deal of current research concerning plants and their energy fields. When plants are in proximity to one another, they can pull energy from each other, which enhances their ability to thrive. I believe that the same thing happens to people. There are people we encounter who feed off our energy to provide what they subconsciously think they're in need of, and we often do the same thing in return. The problem is that this behavior prevents us from being able to achieve our life's purpose. We never fully activate or know how to create with our own energy. Consequently, satisfying relationships are possible only when they're based on mutual understanding and respect on an energetic level.

Awareness of ourselves and the space we occupy is the first step along the path to realizing our life's true purpose. The next step is to master our attention. *Where our attention goes, our energy flows*. To direct and retrieve the energy that we send out and that we need in return, we must focus on, and have control of, our attention. Setting the intention that ultimately leads to achieving our goal of a better life depends on this.

The horizontal plane feels alive, but it really isn't. It's not truth; it's a distorted reality based in duality. It's where our minds drive our attention outward so that we see the world as separate and divided instead of unified and whole.

Feeling tired and unable to complete projects? Failing to create change in your life? To create something new, you need energy. Often, though, many of us have unknowingly given our energy to people and situations in our past and never retrieved it from them. We wait for them to give it back to us in the form of love or validation, but often it never arrives. As a result, we're operating with an empty gas tank because we've given all of our energy away. To realize your life's true purpose, you must retrieve your energy from the people and situations you have given it to so that you can use it to create the life you desire. Otherwise, they will use *your* energy to create *their* reality. The tools described in this chapter will help you retrieve your energy.

Where our attention goes, our energy flows. The creative process is one that involves our attention drifting out of our space. It takes us out to a new field of energy and information, but when we don't know how to bring our attention back, we get stuck outside ourselves and become ungrounded. This chapter is about focusing your attention so that you can discover where your energy is stuck, and then pulling it back into your space so that you can use it to create.

Attention is a great detective. When we pay attention, we know what's going on. When we know what's going on, we know how to find what we need to clear our Backspace and bring our energy back into our own lives.

Client Story

My client Jake is good-looking. He's in his early fifties and a previously successful businessman going through a divorce involving child custody. At the time that he came to me, his life was a trainwreck. His divorce, which was economically exhausting him, had already left him virtually insolvent. His ex-wife was a substance abuser, and although he had been awarded custody of their children, she, with help from her family, was constantly dragging him back to court. To make matters worse, his career had fallen apart, and his relationship with the new woman in his life had just ended.

Jake had, to a great extent, married his parents in the person of someone who combined their negative qualities and brought along an extended family, comparable to his uncles, who created drama and made things worse for Jake. His core Backspace Picture was that of ending up like his father and his uncles, but because he's honest by nature, Jake was chronically unable to move forward. His great ability to succeed was always being stymied, subverted, and reversed by the fear of losing everything.

When I met Jake in the midst of this situation, he had been unemployed and unable to find work. He was old enough to be considered a has-been in his business, and he bought into this Picture. His attention was being pulled apart by the divorce, by his reactions to his upbringing, and by many other things as well. I began my consultations with him by phone, but he was unable to focus or even complete a sentence. He was good at responding to written correspondence, however, so that is how we began our work together.

The first thing I had Jake do was locate his attention as a means of finding his energy. I started to have him ask, out loud, the question, "Where is my attention?" About 40 percent of his attention was on trying to resolve his divorce. Another 40 percent was on trying to create a new career. The balance of his attention was stuck in his Backspace Picture of losing everything and dying alone, like his father.

So much of his energy had been displaced by the divorce that it was difficult for him to bring it back. So instead of focusing his attention outwardly, I had him start focusing on opening to the Wisdom of the Heart. He was not used to returning his energy to himself, which, in turn, caused him to be in a constant state of energy depletion, disabling him from completing his divorce.

I had him imagine his attention as a ball of energy. Jake had a beloved golden retriever, his true companion and unconditional friend. I had him imagine that he was throwing a ball of his "attention/energy" out for his dog to retrieve and that the dog would then find the ball and bring it back. This exercise became Jake's EnergyWorks practice, and it taught him to complete his energy circuit.

Within two months of bringing his attention and energy back in this way, Jake had trained his mind and Heart to act in relationship, sending his attention out and bringing his energy back, and his divorce was completed. All that Jake had to do was repeat the words, "Bring my energy back. Bring my energy back. Bring my energy back." Once he started to repeat these words, his energy returned to him.

Over the next few months, new energy came into Jake's body. He looked years younger, and firms were outbidding each other to hire him. He was soon hired by a top firm in his field.

Next, we worked on Jake's relationships, which involved constant fighting and making up. He now has a calm and stable relationship with an outstanding, independent woman. Most importantly, he's released all drama from his life and has been able to consistently match the frequency of the harmony and new possibilities that now surround him.

Client Story

My client Terry has a coworker who was putting in extra hours on weekends. Terry's boss, a woman, installed cameras at the office and confided in Terry that she didn't trust anyone who chose to work on Saturdays, going so far as to accuse Terry's coworker of stealing money. Terry responded by asking her boss why she had not spoken directly to the accused, angering her boss for making such a suggestion.

At this point, Terry's life included a husband who was putting pressure on her and a close friend who was making unwanted demands. Now she feared for her job. In this critical instant, Terry took a look at where she had been directing her attention and identified several areas outside herself in which other people's energy had been filling her space. She told her boss, firmly, that if she had a problem with another employee, she needed to talk to that person directly and not bring the issue to her. She chose, in that moment, not to allow her boss's energy of mistrust to intrude on her own reality—a condition that, in fact, had been imposed on her by her parents during her upbringing, and by others.

As a regular practice, whenever Terry *retrieved* her energy, she would *receive* it by imagining it as a ball, squeezing it in her Heart like a sponge and saying, "I receive back my energy, and I give back that other person's energy in return." Terry was reclaiming her space, and by doing so, she was making it available as a place for her to create the unknown.

It is essential for our well-being that we live exclusively in our own Heart-space instead of allowing other people's reality to live in us. The following EnergyWorks method provides the steps designed to keep our attention on track.

ENERGYWORKS METHOD
Mastering Attention and Getting Your Energy Back

1. ***Find it.*** Discover where you have given your energy to something or someone and start to pull it back into your own space. To create something new, you need to find your energy and bring it back into your body so that you have enough energy to create a new reality. You can only create with the amount of energy you have access to within your space. Remember, start with what you know you don't want. Then identify what you do want. Then unify the two, move to your center, and be open to something new. Say out loud, "I unify the two and am open to something new!" When you give your energy to others, your energy becomes scattered. Suddenly, you can no longer complete projects, your hopes and dreams are unable to manifest, and you run out of gas because your space is not full. Other people are constantly running their energy through us as a way of getting us to create for them. Therefore, many of us move our attention outside of our space by focusing on others, but we don't bring it back to our Hearts, and our energy, as a result, doesn't create for us. Instead, it creates for them. Your attention is a great detective. It may lead you to old projects or relationships, into your past, into your future, into the negative, or into the positive.

   One of my clients hadn't seen her husband in ten years. I ascertained through our conversation in my office that her attention, many years earlier, had driven her energy to create this marriage in the first place and that the energy still resided there. She didn't believe me; she thought she was over her husband, and this was true, except that she had never pulled her energy back from him. Remarkably, after we pulled her energy back to her Heart, he called her during our session. He could feel her energy leave his space, and he called without any knowledge whatsoever about what we were doing. He had been feeding off, and creating with, her energy all along. His energy had simultaneously remained in her, and this was why she couldn't create a new relationship. Have you given your attention to someone else? Many people don't have the experience of flow in their relationships. Their energy gets stuck in other people's spaces because they're waiting for that other person to return it, meaning that they're waiting for someone else to love them or pay attention to them or validate them, but that never happens. When there is no flow and the energy doesn't come back to you, you need to get it back yourself. By contrast, when you direct your attention to being in relationship with the vertical plane (Source and Earth), it always returns back to you, and an unlimited supply of abundant energy is constantly flowing there, representing miracles and something new and life itself. The horizontal plane feels alive, but it really isn't. It's not true; it's a distorted reality based in duality.

2. ***Retrieve it.*** When our attention takes our energy out of our space and gives it to someone else, we can feel trapped, depleted, isolated, or anxious. I often imagine a guide dog or retriever enlisted to track down my energy. There is a natural tendency

to complete a circuit, so I imagine that my retriever will find the energy wherever it resides and bring it back to my space so that I can start to create. I imagine calling my retriever back, carrying my energy ball to my Heart. To retrieve your energy, move your attention back to your Heart. Imagine your Heart is the target. Your Heart is like a magnet, which, when opened, will automatically attract your energy back. When you place your attention on yourself, your energy will get pulled in like the tide, and light will return to you. You will no longer be sitting in the dark. The Heart is also like a drain in a bathtub—the more you open your Heart, the more your energy will be pulled back into your body like a whirlpool, draining out and down what you don't want from the tub so that you can be filled up with YOUR energy and essence. Many people find it hard to focus on themselves because it's easier to be outer-focused. When you find your energy, move it back to the Heart to complete the circuit. Once the energy returns, you can actively create movement in your space. The more you put attention on your energy within, your energy fields start to spin, and your energy starts to return to you. Say out loud, "Attention Within and Spin!" All you need to do is call your energy back, and it will happen.

3. ***Receive it.*** Imagine filling yourself up with Spirit's energy. Allow that energy to come in through your crown, spiraling downward, into the center of your Heart. Then, from the opposite direction, allow Earth energy to come up through your feet and into the base of your spine, through your central channel

and into your Heart. Visualize these two fields overlapping in your Heart, which will create the eye of your Heart so that you can see and create from Wholeness.

Journaling

Let your mind wander and see where your attention goes. Journaling for at least five minutes will identify where your energy is stored or stuck. Just being aware of where your attention goes can release and set your energy free so that you can create your Intentions. Once you have your list, use the tools from the preceding EnergyWorks Method for each person and situation to call back your energy from those people and places. You can only create with the amount of energy that you have access to in your space. Focus on your heart and say out loud, "I call my energy back." Then say, "Above and below, activate the vortex of flow."

Body Movement

Get a ball or object and hold it in your hand. Connect your thoughts (your attention) to the object so that you make it concrete (as opposed to imagining a false reality not based in concrete form). Say, "I find it." Now that you've found where your energy was stuck, retrieve it and bring it back to your Heart by saying, "I retrieve it." Then put the ball or object against your Heart, squeeze it like a sponge, and say, "I receive it." This movement exercise trains the body to not separate from its energy, but instead to be in relationship with it. If your attention goes into some other reality, not based in the now (such as thinking about a relationship you don't have or something you want), bring your attention back into the object. We want to create a circuit of finding it, retrieving it, and receiving it. If you don't have the energy to move, the tendency is to develop addictive behaviors of all kinds.

5

My Grandmother's Garden: Setting a Space to Create In

My first experience of being connected to Nature was in my grandmother's garden. There, my brother and I would make up games. We would travel to faraway lands where our imaginations could roam wild and free, just like Dorothy's visit to the Land of Oz and Alice's visit to Wonderland. Everything talked to us: the plants, flowers, trees, birds, caterpillars, butterflies, and ladybugs. We would name each one, and we talked to and played with them in our imaginary landscape.

My grandmother taught me how to clear the land in her garden to set the space needed to create something new by planting seeds deep within the soil of Mother Earth, just like the bulldozers at the city dump that cleared and created space. I'd cram a bunch of seeds into one area, but my grandmother quickly pointed out that each individual seed needed space to grow; otherwise, the space, being overfilled, could not give life to any new growth. Likewise, if you list one million intentions in your journal, there isn't enough ground for them to grow in because you have overloaded your space. In your dream space, you can do this, but to manifest anything in the physical realm, you must have enough space.

For some of the seeds I planted with my grandmother, we'd create a mound that was shaped like a bubble. When we planted the seeds, my grandmother would tell me to make a wish and plant the wish in the ground with a seed. I thought that at least some of my wishes would have to come true because I planted so many. I would water my grandmother's garden every day and watch the seeds sprout and then bear fruit.

Eventually, my grandmother and I would pull up the carrots and the turnips, and she would point to the roots. She said the roots of the things we grew were a place of making connection to the Earth. It was a natural explanation of feeling grounded and connected and in relationship with the garden and with the dirt. I would talk to the plants as if they were friends, and intuitively I'd feel connected to this magical garden where there was an overabundance of growth.

I used to eat the raspberries right off my grandmother's raspberry bush, still leaving plenty with which to make raspberry jam for breakfast. I loved lying on the lawn next to the garden. My grandmother lived in Portland, Oregon, and I'd look at the sky and watch the clouds form into different shapes. Have you ever noticed that when you ask the sky a question, it will give you an answer in the form of a cloud, shaped in a particular way? For example, when I asked the sky, "What do you have to tell me today?" the sky always responded with a cloud shaped like a lion or an angel, morphing into different forms representing what I most needed to see. It gave me the feedback I needed to feel loved and supported. Nature will always respond to you so that you know you are not alone.

Often, birds would fly across the sky, and as they moved, I'd feel connected to the universe. Just observing the world around me made me feel calm and relaxed. Ladybugs would land on my hand, and I'd find caterpillars crawling on the leaves. I was in the present moment, connected to all things. I was in the NOW. There was no time nor space.

In my grandmother's garden I used to pull the weeds. The weeds seemed to grow even faster than the plants. They were like the old mental Pictures that I had to keep pulling out and moving into the compost pile in my Backspace. We chose what we wanted to grow, and daily we pulled out what we needed to discard.

Years later, I wrote my college thesis about later-life transitions. I used a garden to describe the different stages, in this case based on the four seasons. I wrote about clearing the space, getting the soil ready, planting and watering the seeds, bringing in the fruit of the harvest, and finally, in winter, when we rest, leaving the soil fallow. The four stages of transition (getting the soil ready and planting the seed, followed by birth and new growth, followed by harvest, and lastly by death and rest) I came to see as a universal cycle. Our Intentions move through the exact same cycles.

In my current life, I sit in my garden every day with bare feet and connect to the Earth. This is a natural way for me to find my space, as I also imagine connecting to the golden sun above. I spend my day on the phone speaking with clients, and most of the time I'm doing this in my garden, which is a space where energy can flow and where I can help my clients create their Intentions.

A bay window in our shower looks out onto my garden, and one day my husband, while taking a shower, observed me out there as I was meditating. My husband said that he saw me as if for the first time and that I looked wonderfully attractive in my garden. He felt that he was looking in on me, as opposed to out at me, and that something shifted for him. Ever since that day he's responded to me differently. Before then, he hadn't really seen me except through his own Pictures and his own past. But when he looked at me that day through the glass and saw me in the garden, he could see my energy connected to the natural world and moving in a magical way, and it changed our relationship. In that moment, my energy was running vertically.

When you are grounded and connected to Nature, you are a reflection of your own true nature. Being in Nature connects you to your own internal Spirit and essence. By contrast, being in the world, you become overtaken by other people's energies and environments and become anxious and overwhelmed and sick because it is no longer your energy you are experiencing, but that of others in your own body. When you don't feel good, it's not your energy. The easiest way to remedy this is to get into Nature so that you understand how your energy actually runs in your own body. You get rid of the energy that is not your own. The more you do this, the more you will be committed to this process. Your personal, true Intentions can only be created with your own energy, never with the energy of someone else.

When I'm in my garden, I'm a creator. I feel like a little girl who has fun and plays, and my imagination is inspired. I approach my life with a playful energy that feeds my Spirit, and this is a way that I can tap into the unknown and bring new tools into my realm. And, like the planet's, your ability to create has no limit. By imagining the space around us as a garden in which to create, we can plant our Intentions in a fertile soil in which they'll grow and thrive. But beware, once you leave your own personal Garden of Eden, which is the Garden Within, you can no longer manifest your Intentions because you are now in the desert, just like Adam and Eve when they were cast out of their garden, and forced to live in the horizontal plane of duality of bad and good and future and past.

When we're stuck in the mind, our attention brings us outside the Garden of Eden (the Garden Within, also known as the void, the space in between, the NOW, the zero point) and, as a result, our energy is directed in a linear way that stops all movement and play. This is the state in which we've all been programmed to follow our thoughts sequentially to get things done. It's the linear place where we're taught that if only we work hard enough, we'll succeed. The Heart, however, creates a circular space around us—a bubble in which we can play. The bubble is the playground in which we're free to move. It's the space in which we truly create.

Through the EnergyWorks Method, I teach my clients to play and, through this process, to create new realities. The ability to play opens up the imagination. It invigorates the soul, it stimulates nerve growth, it shapes the brain, and it helps process emotions. Play nourishes our Spirit, and by opening up our imagination, it gives us our most powerful tool for creating, stimulating, and exploring a new reality. The more we can imagine and play with a new reality that we seek to create, the more we can bring things into manifestation on the physical plane.

The way to create something new is through the imagination, and the ability to spontaneously create occurs when the Heart and the imagination connect. The Garden Within is the place where I make this connection, and being committed to it is my source of unity. In my garden I am free to do and create whatever I want. This is what we all long for—this is what makes us happy. When I engage in play, life is always new, and it fills me up.

The Garden Within is a place for us to play and feel free to let go of ourselves. When we let go of Pictures of who we are, we let go of the ego and the known so that we can create from the unknown. When we are immersed in playing in our garden, we are in an unrestrained state of being, and we can experience happiness, joy, laughter, and fun. This promotes our ability to bring our dreams to reality.

My clients come to me filled with confusion and stress. They are outside their own space, due to their own negative judgments of themselves, as well as other people's condemnation and criticism, causing them to intellectualize how things "should be," which stops them from moving and playing. They have been programmed to live outside of their space, in the dry, arid desert, where there is no energy and only snakes and scorpions thrive. And they don't know why they can't create. Someone else in their lives has taken over their energy and space, and they wonder why they cannot manifest their Intentions. They are in what is known as the Game of Survival and getting things done in a linear fashion. They believe in effort and competition and sometimes even revenge, and they focus their attention on others and the external world, keeping them disconnected and unable to access the beautiful gardens within them. But the more fun they have, and the more they can just be in their own space, the more my clients and I can create together.

Client Story

When Tina first came to see me, she told me all about her alcoholic, narcissistic mother. For years and years, Tina's attention had been focused on her mother (as is almost always the case with children of narcissists). And her attention was always in the future. How could it be otherwise, when she was always directing her attention outside of herself and her inner garden to the external world where her mother lived? Ironically, Tina's mother wanted to have a relationship with someone, as did Tina, and Tina soon found her mother flirting with her boyfriends because Tina's mother was in competition with her. As a result, my client's attention was far in the future, worrying about what was going to happen and what her mother was going to do to prevent disasters that hadn't even happened yet. Tina lived outside her garden. She was trying to prevent her mom from interfering in her life. On Tina's birthdays, her mom would get drunk and stir up drama and chaos. The moment Tina got close to anyone, her mom would go on a drinking binge, forcing Tina to once again turn her full attention to her mom, thereby destabilizing her new relationship and any chance of happiness.

With her attention outside of herself, Tina was always full of anxiety and fear and became ungrounded, and she would destroy her relationships with new men because she was chaotic herself from having to try to manage her mom's chaos. She frightened her new boyfriends away.

Tina was always playing the Game of Survival to stay safe, but because she was focused outside of her garden, only chaos was created. All of her relationships were doomed to failure. When she started to focus her attention inward on the Garden Within, everything started to grow and thrive. Three major events happened with her mother that Tina refused to give any attention to. That is when Tina showed up for herself and a new guy showed up for her. My husband and I went to Tina's wedding, and my husband actually said, "Wow, Tina's new husband really loves her." My husband saw the energy Tina's new husband was emitting. When you live in your garden, your energy can be seen. When you are living outside your garden, people cannot see you because nothing is growing. It's all desert, false realities, and mirages.

The following EnergyWorks Method provides the steps, in detail, to incorporate the power of play in creating a new reality and accessing the Garden Within to achieve your goals.

ENERGYWORKS METHOD

1. ***Create a space to play in.*** The Garden Within is your playground. It is just like a baseball field, basketball court, swimming pool, or garden—even like a video game or virtual space that you can play in. Focusing on your Heart creates a bubble around you that consists of a magnetic field generated by the Heart. Think of it as extending about three and a half feet on each side of you. To create anything, you must first create space within you; otherwise, you can't create. If you allow other energies to invade your space, you won't have space.

2. ***Set your space.*** Once you have created a bubble to play in, you need to set the space around you. The bubble around you is not empty. It is filled with energy and information. You need to know what's yours and what's not yours. To create a new reality, you need to set the space at a vibration like joy or peace. Let the Heart be represented by a diamond and draw a diamond in the center of the bubble. Choose a color and an emotion that you want to be in. By setting your space, you'll know who you are, so you won't lose yourself when you play with others. Setting your space gives you the ability to know how to move through space and time.

3. ***Play with attention to the goal.*** Playing is about focusing your attention on an activity or an action as you are moving through the horizontal plane so that you remain in the vertical plane. When you play, you are focused on doing some activity with a goal that you are playing to. Even if your goal is of the imagination, it entails a particular focus. Your attention is your ability to play by focusing and moving your energy toward that goal, like moving a ball around the field to score.

4. ***Play with movement.*** Imagine a group of kids playing. They jump into a game and make things up as they go along, taking whatever action they can visualize toward reaching their goals to keep the game moving forward. If that doesn't work, they take another action, and in the process, they might invent something completely new. But they never lose sight of the goal that they're playing to. It's the movement in a space that gets your attention. You

are learning how to move your Spirit in a body. By creating this movement, you are creating a ***Unified Field***, and that's when miracles happen, as opposed to being separate and divided.

5. ***Play with fun.*** When you're having fun daily, your goals come into manifestation. Here is a good example of this: My ten-year-old son was very serious about hitting a baseball, but he had been approaching the problem under stress and not having success. I came unannounced to his batting practice, wearing butterfly wings and calling myself the batting fairy. As I watched him at the plate, I noticed that his attention was all over the place. With the coach's permission, I told my son, as he stood up to the plate, to focus on the tip of his nose, pulling his attention into his space, and then to project the diamond of his Heart out in front of him to see the ball in the strike zone. The batting fairy was in the Picture to make the process fun, and kids tend to learn faster because they are able to move in play. My son started smashing the ball, as did his teammates, and the coach wound up thanking me for bringing play into a game that had become too serious. The point is: Keep focused inwardly, which creates the space for you to play, so that you become unaffected by what people think and do and they can no longer get into your space.

6. ***Play your way into a new reality.*** When you feel isolated, alone, anxious, or depressed, you're in a distorted mental Picture, and the quickest way to get out of it is to play your way out. When you have a problem at work, in a relationship, or in any

> other tough situation, instead of working harder and overanalyzing and remaining overly serious, play your way out. When you bump up against negative energy, ask your body how it wants to play. Start to move your body. Start to run or jump or dance. If you don't know how to play, watch some kids. There's movement, spontaneity, imagination, and endless alternatives to getting caught. Playing a game with someone else will help you feel more connected and increase your creativity. Play is a way we can move through our space that changes our reality. We get stuck when we forget to have fun. To create a new reality, we have to be in our space like a child with endless possibilities—imagining, exploring, moving in fun, and feeling free. When you are immersed in play, you get lost. It's in getting lost that answers come in and through. Getting lost creates a new path and a new reality, because when you are lost in play, you have no past and no future.

A joyful spontaneity and sense of freedom would affect me every time I entered my grandmother's garden. This feeling continues in my own garden today. When I connect to the Earth, I can move my energy down and move the seeds of my Intention into the soil. Through these connections, my roots remain solid.

We can experience the same type of spontaneous creation in the ground of the natural world. In a forest, there is a mother tree. It is through her roots, embedded with the microbes in the Earth, that connection, communication, and relationship with trees thousands of miles away take place. Upon death, the mother tree passes on her information and her energy, ensuring the survival of, and prolonging the lives of, the things around her, and thus she becomes a part of the interconnected web of life.

The Garden of Eden can be seen as a story about Adam and Eve living in a paradise of unity. Everything was whole and complete, and they experienced the complete flow of things in a pure state of being. When the serpent came into the garden, it gave them a Picture of a new way of living based in the mind. When we live in the mind, duality is created. Separation is created. Right and wrong are created.

It is my belief that we've been programmed out of being in our own inner gardens. We've been searching outside of ourselves for a connection and a sense of unity only to find ourselves separated and disconnected. We blindly seek to return to a garden of peace, pure being, and possibility, which we cannot see because we are not sitting in the eye of our Hearts. Only there is creation possible. It is in and from the Heart that things are created spontaneously.

When we work from the mind, we feel uprooted from the natural world around us. We look for ways to fill the holes in our lives and connect with the people around us, but what we usually find instead are entanglements, chaos, and confusion because we are not connected vertically to our Source. Nor are we rooted in the Earth.

So, to find the Garden of Eden within, you must occupy your Heart. Your Heart is the space from which you will experience a new evolutionary jump. By occupying your Heart, you bring in the unknown, and a new reality can be created instantaneously. You must know how to move and play in your garden so that your network of relationships will expand like roots that connect you to the people around you, so that they, too, can experience the same spontaneous shift. It is through this connection, communication, and relationship that something greater comes about.

Journaling

Identify where you don't have space in your life. Then ask yourself why. List all the reasons you don't have space in your life. Are you a codependent people pleaser? Are you a martyr for your children? Do you give up your space to heal everyone else around you? Who is in your space? Ask yourself, "Who is in my space?" and watch who shows up in your space during your day. Once you identify who is showing up, ask yourself, "Do I really need to be expending my energy in this way?" Then say, "I return my attention within and spin." This is about learning who you are creating for. Am I creating for me or for someone else? Usually, when people create something, they have to run it through someone else. We have to shut the door on allowing others to run their energy through us so that we end up creating for them and not for ourselves.

Body Movement

Draw a bubble and look at the empty space within the bubble. Fill up the bubble with two colors and write down what energy you want to feel and be vibrating at. Get up and breathe those colors in and out (one color on the in-breath and the other color on the out-breath) and return to those colors throughout the day as you move through your day.

6

The Power of Filling Up

My husband was a Golden Gloves champion boxer and an outstanding all-around athlete. When he was in his late forties, he was playing semi-pro ball with college players and professionals, including former Major Leaguers. He was used to having a strong body, and coming from an Italian background, he's strong headed and has a quick temper as well.

My husband had hated his job of over twenty years but had convinced himself to keep doing it to support his family. Partly as a result of that, he's grown to associate receiving money with doing things that don't bring pleasure. He's volunteered as a baseball coach over the years and has been generous with his time, giving hundreds of hours and helping kids in Little League and high school. But he's rejected the suggestion of getting paid for this work that he loves because of being convinced that payment would automatically make the work obligatory and remove the pleasure he derives.

This notion of giving and refusing to receive back kept his life off balance. It's as though he was exhaling all the breath out of his body and having no energy left to inhale. Without the movement of energy in both directions, our lives can't move, and this throws us out of whack. In my husband's case, this sense of being out of whack was manifested at home and in every other phase of his life. He was constantly giving without receiving in return.

Seven years ago, my husband injured himself while playing baseball. He was in so much pain that he had to start taking painkillers, and this is when he took a turn for the worse. He started to drop into depression, and his nerve pain didn't cease. His doctors found out that he had a cyst in his spinal cord and two herniated disks. My father had lived with the same injury, so my husband's condition brought up images of my childhood. I was looking at my husband laid out flat on the floor in pain just like my father had been when I was growing up.

My husband couldn't work for more than eight months. When I was young, I had gone on overdrive to support my family, and now I had to do the same. I'm a healer by nature and profession, but my husband refused my healing work because he didn't want to be fixed. I had to give him his space and observe him, acknowledging as I did so that each person has to decide their own path. A person must go into agreement with any healer or healing process before it can be given or received, and my husband's inability to receive in general prevented him from asking for and receiving help.

I knew my foundation was falling apart. Everything I'd built for my family up to this point had to be let go, and I had to watch it fall. I could even see how these changes affected my children. My sons were not used to seeing their father, so masculine and strong, show his vulnerable side, and they tried to heal him in their own ways. My older son, who was twelve at the time, set up a massage business. He ordered hot stones and a massage table, and created therapeutic lotions that he could use on his dad to heal him. I also showed my son some techniques of laying on of hands, and my husband's resistance began to soften.

Finally, my husband asked me if I could help him. This request was more about him opening up and being receptive to his own feminine healing energy within. I performed a hands-on healing. I said, "Imagine receiving the inhale in everything you do. For example, say, 'I am receiving water, I am receiving food, and I am receiving a walk.' If you can make your daily life focused on receiving and moving your energy inward, then you will come back to life."

It's so easy to give to others, to help people, to volunteer without wanting anything in return, but you must receive your energy back. This simple act of focusing inward and filling up will allow you to give and receive for *yourself* by activating the circle of flow. If you only give, it's not truly giving because there is no self-care. To fill yourself up, you must open up to receive.

My husband then began to be creative, a process that up till then he had never pursued, and it was through imaginative projects that led to creating art that he was able to heal and create a new life. He bought and started to assemble small metal puzzles of tanks, planes, and military objects. He moved on to bending clothes hangers and using duct tape to fashion Disney characters like Mickey Mouse that could be wall mounted. He then hand-wove brilliantly colored baseball gloves. He built a large replica of the Golden Gate Bridge for our sons to wear as a costume for Halloween. And he sewed Captain America (how symbolic is that?) leather backpacks. He had created out of chaos. From the chaos, through creativity, he created his way out of pain and out of a chaotic situation and started to change his life, reinforcing that you can indeed create your way out of chaos.

I could see that by getting in touch with his creative side, my husband was using his pain and the depression as fuel to create a new life for himself. It was through art that he was creating his new life, and as he used his imagination to create things, his life became more mysterious and unexpected things started to happen. He began to experience synchronicity and receive communication from the natural world.

One day a squirrel showed up in my garden. It came right over to where I was sitting and just looked at me. Then it walked a little farther, sniffed a dandelion in the grass, and finally just walked off. Later that day, my husband reported that a squirrel had come into the garage, looked at him, and then gone back outside. The next morning he had the hood of his car opened, when a squirrel jumped up, sat on top of the battery, and refused to budge. He had to get on the road, so he shut the hood and assumed that the squirrel would jump off as soon as the engine started. He drove across the Golden Gate Bridge, then into downtown San Francisco to a big parking garage, and wondered when he got out if the squirrel could still possibly be in the car. Sure enough, he lifted the hood and the squirrel was sitting there looking at him. My husband was a little disconcerted as he wondered what the squirrel was going to do in the heart of the city, but at five o'clock when he came back to the garage and looked under the hood, there was the squirrel waiting for a ride home. They drove back over the Golden Gate Bridge and back to our house, after which the squirrel hung out with my husband for about a week and a half and then was gone. My husband would talk to the squirrel during that time and felt connected to it.

The squirrel was a sign to my husband of a change in his life and situation. He had been dealing with debilitating health problems, and the episode with the squirrel was like a miracle because he had never been in communication with animals or with the natural world. The space around him filled with a brand-new energy, and playing in that space presented him with a whole new reality. To this day, my husband takes a daily walk in Nature.

These days, I fill up my home space as a way of keeping my family at ease in the world. I want them to come home to an experience of light and the Garden Within and to be able to drop the energy that they've been subjected to and programmed by during the day. I do this by visualizing a Diamond in the center of my home to represent their true nature and remind them who they are. I ground to the planet as a way of clearing and transforming. I then connect up to Source and the Unified Field above, bringing the energy and information from the planet and the Unified Field together into the Diamond in my home. I ask Source to cleanse my home and ask for the light to fill it up.

If we're already filled with the energy of the planet and with Spirit, we won't allow people to dump their junk in our personal space and play out their energetic patterns. But if we are half-empty, we can allow people to overtake us because we're often afraid that we won't have friends or be loved. Often people continue to accept the negative energy of others because they want to avoid being alone. We also forgo focusing inwardly and taking care of ourselves because we are focused on the needs of others.

Do you put other people's needs before your own? If you do, this behavior is a form of abandonment. We often give to other people what we need to give to ourselves, but bringing these things back to ourselves is an important form of receiving. We have been programmed out of thinking about filling ourselves up with our own attention and energy; we've been made to feel uncomfortable or selfish about the idea of giving to ourselves. In reality, this attention to our own inner world is exactly what we need to thrive.

In every moment, when you ask yourself the question, "What can I do for myself or what do I need?" the asking, by itself, will begin the process of allowing you to receive. The EnergyWorks Method is about connection, communication and co-creation. It is something that you don't have to work hard at doing.

When I feel my life being swept away in the horizontal wave of the chaos of the world around me, I simply ask the planet to ground me and empty me out. I ask Spirit to connect me and empty me out. Then I ask the planet and the stars to fill me up. Just by asking, you receive.

Our body is like the proverbial glass. Our energy is like water. When our glass is full, we see our lives that way. When it's empty, we do the same. The important thing to know is that we have the power to fill ourselves up, and when we're filled with our own energy, we're able to create. This chapter is about giving your energy and attention to the light within and not giving that light away. It's about self-esteem and confidence and recognizing the value of the light within you. It's about being able to elevate yourself and the world around you as a result.

Client Story

My client Jane is the mother of a two-year-old girl. When she came to me, she was pregnant again and desperately wanted a boy. Jane's grandfather, with whom she'd been close all her life, was dying, and he had reinforced her anxiety by telling her for years that the way to have a perfect family was to produce a girl and then a boy. The older girl could then assist in the boy's care, which according to the grandfather, was paramount.

In the beginning stages of her new pregnancy, Jane felt strongly that she was having her longed-for boy. She began talking to her unborn child with that in mind, and even went so far as to start buying male-oriented toys. She went further still by assuring her grandfather that she was having a boy. When he asked her how she knew, Jane answered that she just did.

Then after the initial stages of the pregnancy, Jane found out that she was, in fact, having another girl. From the moment the doctor gave her the news, Jane was devastated and cried uncontrollably. Her grandfather had passed by then, and she felt in some way that she was disappointing him and had broken the promise of a boy in the family. She was conflicted because, though she knew that even the ability to have a baby is a blessing, she was feeling incomplete. Furthermore, a part of her felt disconnected because she'd been wrong in the face of such personal certainty.

To shed light on Jane's issues, I decided to have her create a movie. I had her describe the scene when the doctor called, and I had her describe the setting she was in. I had her describe the characters that showed up and how they responded to the situation. Beginning at the point where her expectations were shattered, I had her move from the doctor's phone call at the start of the scene, to the end of the scene, when she called her husband, who had also been disappointed. Then, when the next scene proceeded with her husband telling her parents about the sex of the baby, something new was revealed. In that moment Jane remembered her own birth and the story that had unfolded when her parents had found out that she was a girl.

Prior to her birth, Jane's parents had thought that she was going to be a boy, and the first words that her mother said to her father in the aftermath of Jane's birth were "I'm sorry." In the ensuing years, my client lived through incident after incident of not being seen, not even existing. Communication by her family from early on, even in the womb, was directed not to her, but to a boy.

We moved Jane through the preceding steps and created a new Picture of energy and information where she was seen and acknowledged, and where the first words coming from her mother at her birth were "I love you." We then fast-forwarded to Jane's current situation and created a new Picture of the moment she found out she was giving birth to a daughter, having her respond this time by saying, "I love you." We then reshot the scene of her telling her grandfather that she was having a little girl, but this time in a spirit of embracing feminine creative energy. We established new Pictures of connection and communication with the little girl still in Jane's belly. Through this process, my client laid full claim to her female creative energy and her power. Her pregnancy was no longer about having a boy or girl. It was about Jane being filled and about her being connected to both her masculine and feminine, transcending gender and validating the spirit in the baby's body. Jane was freed from the programming in her family that had made her want her baby to be one sex or another. I had her physically plant seeds in her home garden to represent a new foundation for both her existing and her new family. Now, the whole family is filled.

When you focus on your Heart, the Heart creates a bubble around you. That is the container for your Spirit's energy and Mother Earth's energy to fill you up. When this happens, you will know the purpose of why you are here. And if you are unable to balance your masculine and feminine energies within, you will try to do so externally.

ENERGYWORKS METHOD

1. ***Ask the planet to empty you out.*** To fill up with your own energy, you must first empty out. To empty out, you have to ground yourself. *Grounding yourself is like pulling the plug in a bathtub so that all of the energy and information you are sitting in moves out.*

2. ***Ask Spirit to empty you out.*** Ask Spirit to help you remember who you are and what you came here to do. By focusing on Spirit, you are in truth. By focusing on Spirit, you have the ability to create and tap into unlimited possibilities. For most of us, what we create is the direct result of our programming by others in our space. Here, we ask Spirit to empty us of all beliefs that came from our genetic line, our parents, and our environment, of who we were programmed to believe we were meant to be. The only way to know who you are is to focus on Spirit. Then you become the effect of Spirit's energy in your space.

3. ***Ask the planet to renew you.*** When you focus on your Heart, your Heart will start to receive the planet's energy and information from the day, and all you need to do is ask the planet to renew you and update you with the energy update. Say, "Update me with the new energy and information so I can grow and thrive in the body in physical form."

4. ***Ask Spirit to fill you up to receive.*** Focus on your Heart and this will open you up. Ask and invite Spirit into your space. Allow Spirit to fill you up with miracles. You want to focus on what Spirit is creating in you today. You want to look at what Spirit is doing in you. By being aware of Spirit and by observing Spirit, you will be set up to receive more than you can imagine. You will be able to create the unknown.

5. ***Activate the Greater Whole.*** When you focus in your Heart, the magnetic field pulls in the above and below, Spirit and planet, to create the eye of your Heart. The eye of your Heart is where two energies come together to create a third energy where something new can be born. It is in this energy that we can experience the Holy Spirit. This is where the masculine and feminine energies overlap. The eye of the Heart enables you to create and birth something from wholeness as opposed to duality.

Journaling

In your journal, ask Spirit to fill you up. Draw a Picture of yourself with a gold sun above your head, and ask Spirit to fill you up with the gold so that you can have miracles enter your space. In the gold sun, write your Intention and fill yourself up. Then trace the outside of your body in your journal with the color gold so that gold is a complete energy circuit around your body.

Body Movement

Imagine the gold sun you just drew is in your Heart and that you are the center of the Universe. Imagine everything moving around you like the planets. There has to be space between you and the planets for the planets to move around you. Stretch your arms out, side to side, and forward and back, and in doing so, define the edges of your space. Inhale inward, with your arms moving upward, to connect to Spirit, and then move your arms out and around to define your field; then move your arms downward to connect to the planet as you exhale. Finally, cross your hands in front of your Heart, with the Earth and Spirit energies, in a form of energetic exchange that you imagine in your Heart.

7

Open to the Wisdom of the Heart

When I was a very young girl, I could see energy in the empty spaces around both people and objects. The energy that I saw looked like white or gold bubbles. When light hit the bubbles, they would sparkle like diamonds. These fields, or bubbles of energy, would move around the people I saw or attach to them. The in-between spaces sometimes looked empty, but then the bubbles would fill them, moving a little bit like soap bubbles in the air, touching together and connecting to form even larger bubbles. Sometimes, I'd rub my eyes, and it seemed as though some kind of film was covering them, like raindrops on a windshield.

I could see other kinds of light, too. I remember looking out my window in the morning and staring into the light. I'd look at the empty space between my house and the tree in my front yard and see the light shimmer like a heatwave rising above a city street on a hot summer's day or a mirage in the desert. It was also like watching a wave at the ocean, but a wave made of light. Watching the energy moving in space comforted me. The adults in the room would say, "Come back to Earth." But I always seemed to remain in my own world of light. It felt so good to drift. I felt as though I was floating like the bubbles. I would imagine that I was inside the bubbles and floating off into the light. I could imagine creating and being in different kinds of worlds that were as real as this world.

This (invisible to others) world of light was always moving, changing, and flowing, and the energy in the empty spaces seemed to change easily, depending on who or what was in the space. I would talk to the light as if it were a person. I thought of the bubbles as angels, and even though my parents were never religious or prayed, I had such a strong connection that I would actually be in constant communication with the light. I believe, based on my own experience, that when children talk to imaginary friends, they are interacting with the energy in this "in-between space." They can see it and feel it.

Down the street from me lived a kindly older gentleman, Mr. Reins, who was taking care of his sick wife. My family knew him, and I would go to church with him every Sunday so that he wouldn't have to go alone. We would do fun activities at church, but what stood out for me were the pictures in the Bible of people with halos. That same light around the head is what I would see in my own world, but the color, often, was black or gray. Out of the corner of my eye, I could also see a purple flashing light, like a purple firefly, except that I could see it during the day. Purple light would move around me, circling my space. When I felt unsafe, I would call on the purple light because I thought of it as a kind of electric fence that would zap anything that threatened me or came too close.

I kept a pet goldfish in a bowl on the table by the living room window, and I'd stare into the bowl for long periods of time. I'd look down into the fishbowl and talk to my pet fish, Charlie. I remember watching Charlie swimming around in the water for hours, and I felt just like him, but instead of swimming in water, I felt as if I were swimming in the space around myself—a space that was moving and flowing just like water. Like the water in the fishbowl, the energy I moved in would change. Sometimes, I felt like I was swimming upstream, and at other times I felt like I was simply floating. I remember wondering if I was just like my fish—swimming in a bowl with someone looking down on me. I wondered if my fish could see the water he was moving through or could only see the physical objects it contained, like the rocks and the fake kelp. The water in the fishbowl was similar to the energy I could see in the "space in between." I not only could see the energy but also could feel it, depending on what energy was in the space, which would affect how I felt.

Moving through this space was easy when the light energy was bright gold, white, teal, blue, and green. I felt calm, peaceful, and happy. At other times, however, I would see dark energy. I would feel sad and scared, and I would cry for no reason. Depending on who or what was in the space, I would feel waves of their energy move through me, and I would experience it as if it were my own. When I was around certain people, the waves felt choppy, and I would get emotional and be unable to calm down. The energy in the empty space sometimes seemed like a tidal wave, generating so much chaos that I'd feel as though I were drowning. I would often feel this way around one of my dad's friends who visited our home. I remember putting Elvis Presley's "Jailhouse Rock" on my little record player and dancing around, when this man suddenly entered my room. As soon as he entered, I stopped moving. My dad's friend was a chain smoker and his hands shook, causing the light to turn dark and making the fun and movement disappear.

The energy in the space around me would change depending on who was in my "fishbowl." I remember going to a friend's house up the street. Her father would drink a lot and then get angry. I'd see a red energy and feel it hitting me like a wave. I'd feel his anger surge through me and wonder what I'd done wrong. I always got blamed for something in the midst of this, and I bought into the fact that I was responsible for it. When I felt this energy hit me, my friend would change her demeanor and become angry, too. Her parents blamed me for her behavior, as well, and at times like this they'd look at me with judgment and disgust. All of their pain moved into me, and I was somehow convinced that I was at fault. I carried this guilt around with me, day in and day out.

Then, about the time I entered first grade, a family consisting of a single mother and six kids moved in next door. Louise, one of the daughters, was four years older than me, and she soon became my best friend. I would follow her around, and I was happy for her to lead because she was older and was nice to me. Louise was the oddball in her family, and she was similar to me in that she was always the one getting blamed or attacked. She was also very sensitive and intuitive.

Both Louise and I were interested in seeing the light and seeing the world of angels and energy fields. We would play a game that consisted of looking at ourselves in the bathroom mirror until we no longer saw our faces reflected but saw the light that emanated instead. We would also look each other in the eyes and try not to blink until our faces disappeared. Sometimes we would concentrate on the space between us and would tell each other what we saw. We were happy in each other's company, both of us unable to deal with the chaos around us, but secure in the company of another person who could perceive and communicate with light.

Our energy is our greatest resource. It is the source of power that we need to learn how to use so that we can accomplish our goals or create our Intentions. You can't create or destroy energy, but you can change it.

A field of energy contains information and vibration (which you can't create or destroy but can change), and to create our Intentions, we must match and then access the information and vibration of that field. We can create change by using, directing, moving, and transforming energy. When we start to move our energy, things begin to get stirred up; it may feel like we're in a tornado. But we can illuminate the energy that isn't ours and then release it by grounding and connecting to the planet and the Unified Field, after which we can fill up with our own energy and create our Intentions and fulfill our life's purpose.

The Heart creates a wave of energy that moves out and flows in the space around us. I call this the "Heart Wave." The Heart moves like a wave in the ocean. When you feel angry, your Heart Wave, in response, becomes very choppy. When you feel love instead, your Heart Wave is smooth and flows peacefully. In this chapter, you will learn how to choose it, move it, and use it. You also will learn how to set your Heart Wave and let it move throughout your space, throughout your day, so that you can be riding on that wave, as opposed to being taken out by the tsunami of another person's chaotic energy. In addition, you will learn how to cancel the choppy waves of other people's anger, or the undertow of other people's depression and problems that they try to dump in your space for you to fix.

The Heart is an organ of communication, and the other organs of the body follow its responses. Researchers show that human beings can generate light in their hearts by doing Heart-centered meditations. Human beings are made of light energy, and light is the essence of all communication. This communication creates a relationship between what you want and what you don't want, and the Heart is the center of that relationship. In fact, the Greater Whole is created where the energies intersect and a new energy, "the Diamond energy of the Heart," is created.

Our Heart has the ability both to attract matching energy fields and to unify opposing energies. When we learn how to use the energy of magnetism, the vibration of what we want to create starts to multiply. But the energy of the Heart can seem treacherous, especially when the Heart is closed and we experience pain. Pain is a signal that our energy has been hijacked or infiltrated, but when we move our attention to the Heart, our energy returns and fills us up, and the energy of other people in our space leaves.

When we commit to occupy the throne of our Heart, we become Heart-powered. The Heart unifies the Spirit and Body, bringing them into communication and relationship. The Heart pulls in their unique fields of energy, and the overlap creates an energy that is stronger and greater than that which existed when they were separate. I call the space where the Spirit and Body overlap in a separate space the Greater Whole, and the subtle, invisible energy that emerges from this combination creates magnetism. When two fields of energy come together, they can produce something greater than if they were separate and apart. It's a physical, electric, and magnetic energy that has both a positive and a negative charge.

When we open to the ***Wisdom of the Heart***, we can access the energy of the Greater Whole and are then able to create the life we really want. We are like a king or queen commanding energy, and thus we have the advantage of certainty in any situation. But to maintain this combination of the energies of Body and Spirit that makes us Whole and allows us to create, we must occupy the throne of our Heart.

When we learn to open the throne of our Heart, we take up residence in the place where we find our own space and experience peace. It may seem, at times, as if we're on a bucking bull. But if we know where to sit and how to move our energy, we won't be thrown off. We can flow through any situation with ease and grace.

Pictures are created by our state of mind. Are we always focused on what is wrong, as opposed to what is right? Are we observing energy that is not moving, as opposed to that which is? Most people create their Pictures from the brain. They use external Pictures to determine what they want, and they let the external world determine who they are. They have to see something manifested to believe it exists. Even if they can imagine a Picture, they can't create it because it's the movement of the Heart Wave that brings Pictures into reality. So, they're seeing, perceiving, and reacting from a distortion.

The Heart is the electromagnetic center of the body. Its magnetic field is five thousand times stronger than that of the brain. By its very nature, it seeks to be in relationship with the brain. That is why it is so important to use the Heart to create our Intentions. When we put the brain in charge, it tries to overtake or separate from the Heart, putting us in duality, but the Heart wants unity and will bring together the energy fields of the physical Body and subtle energy of Spirit.

All energy contains information, and cells are energetic. Heart cells are electric and magnetic. The Heart is a filter that can override the external world of energy and information. The Heart has highly synchronized cells that are able to use their external energy to increase the amplitude of incoming energy signals. For example, if we are in the vibration of love, that vibration will pull in matching vibrations and multiply that energy. When we are in love and happy and the Heart Wave is moving out in response, everywhere we go people seem to match and move in that Heart Wave, and the state of being happy and in love multiplies. But if we vibrate with negative energy, that energy will attract a negative matching vibration. If negative vibration and information are contained in our mental Pictures and we match their negative energy, that information will surface in our world.

The Heart is like a tuning fork with the power to set the energy around it, and we therefore have a choice between setting the vibration ourselves or matching the vibration others set. It is therefore of paramount importance for us to *set the energy of the Heart* so that it doesn't match vibrations that we don't want to attract. If we set the Heart Wave, it will only respond to that vibration that we set, such as love, and it will pull in matching vibrations that cause love to multiply.

What do we tune our vibration to? Are we tuned into gossip, drama, and problems, or are we tuned into peace, love, and joy? How do we respond to the vibrations around us? Most people believe that the brain initiates a response, but the Heart initiates a response as well. Researchers have shown that meditation can generate visible light energy from the Heart if the technique is Heart-centered. The Heart is the core of our energy field, and if our field changes, it will change the fields of those around us.

The Heart generates light energy that moves in wave patterns. This is how energy sends information and vibration through space and time. The resulting communication affects other light energy around it, so that when we make our own Intentions and set our Heart Wave, others begin to match, move, and use it, changing the vibration and information in the field of energy we've created in their jobs, homes, and relationships.

Energy is information and vibration. It is constantly in communication between the Heart, brain, and body. The vibration of the Heart moves wave patterns to the brain, heightening its emotional state, memory, and well-being. The Heart moves energy in wave patterns that are represented by loops, like the loops we associate with the infinity symbol. By moving energy through these loops, we clear our space.

The Heart transforms energy, which changes the body's response, and the brain is the observer of that energy. The Heart filters, cleans, and directs energy; the brain participates in creating a new reality by observing it, and the body responds to this new reality. Energy always wants to be observed.

The Heart is the magnetic and electric center of the body, and the cells in the Heart are 65 percent neural and identical to those in the brain. The electromagnetic field of the Heart is called the throne of the soul. When we open the Heart and own this space, the Heart Wave will bring the brain into relationship instead of allowing the brain to remain separate. Furthermore, the Heart Wave is able to achieve a higher emotional state of well-being than the brain, and it can block out negative energy fields. The Heart Wave brings things into relationship and facilitates our connection to the Greater Whole.

Client Story

One client I've been working with for a few years has a goal to move her career forward, and her progress has been mainly the result of her newfound ability to neutralize the energy of her husband, a man with an intensely reactive nature. Her husband has a high-powered and highly lucrative job in the financial industry, and because he often worked out of a home office and had an explosive reaction to daily events, she was subjected to, and often derailed by, his constant blowups.

As this situation intensified, his habit of making decisions in a reactive space began to take every aspect of their lives in a negative direction. The husband's business partner embezzled a substantial portion of their funds, creating obvious levels of extreme pressure, and his secretary became mistake-prone as a result of being subjected to his subsequent anger. On a daily basis, this stuck situation was manifested in things like unexpected car breakdowns, lost keys, and countless other minor mishaps. He suffered lost relationships with friends, and in a short amount of time their personal net worth, due to one reactive decision after another, dwindled from millions of dollars to the point where they had to borrow money for a mortgage payment. My client was pushed, through proximity to this energetic drama, into feeling powerless.

Finally, observing her husband literally beginning to go crazy, she decided she'd had enough, and we began to work together on identifying her own Intentions, focusing on her own energy, and turning this chaos around.

At the time that all of this was unfolding, my client was a professor, and her progress in her field and in her department was being constantly stymied by a competitive colleague. In our initial work, we focused on setting her true Intentions and playing to her real Pictures. We identified the mental Pictures she was stuck with and set up a process to redirect her energy. We focused, for the first time in her professional life, on her own true Intentions, as opposed to her husband's or her colleague's. Out of this process, she resigned her position and founded an institute that specializes in her particular field. She is now working internationally with major players, including heads of state, who are embracing the theories and concepts that she began to express when she began our process.

Conversely, her situation at home grew progressively worse. Even with the experience of having blown all of their resources, her husband continued to spew verbal and emotional venom that affected not only my client but also their young children—to the extent that their sleep patterns and overall health were affected. As a result, my client was confronted with the absolute necessity to take action in every phase of her life. She proceeded, without her husband's involvement, to set Pictures of a space of new opportunity for him in his professional field. Several opportunities for renewed financial stability soon became available to him, and he was able to take advantage of them. Her energy had redirected and moved her husband's energy.

Her next step was to identify those mental Pictures of her husband that involved making bad decisions based purely on reaction. He was saddled, as it turned out, with a recent devastating family loss that had been compounded by unexpected financial hardship in its aftermath, and that event had marked the beginning of his worst downward spiral. He had been stuck in the Picture of himself as a member of a family prone to financial disaster, and his genetic line was beginning to play out in him.

My client had to focus on her goals instead of focusing on her husband, like a driver who focuses on the road ahead but glances in the rearview mirror to see what might be approaching from behind. She redirected the negative energy that was pursuing her and used it to move forward. Early on, our bodies learn how to survive. Because my client's husband grew up in an environment of financial instability and constant chaos, his body would not let go of survival strategies. His body was holding onto these survival strategies because, for example, just like in war, if you fall asleep, you might die. Consequently, his body believed that it had to automatically respond as it always had done and react in a certain way, in an effort to keep him alive. Yet, the truth is that this method only kept him alive but did not allow him to grow, change, and thrive.

Incredibly, within a few days of the onset of this work taking place without his direct knowledge or participation, my client's husband expressed verbally to his wife a new Intention, and it was in absolute congruity with the Intention she had set and that he had matched. The possibility then existed that her husband might be able to turn his life around personally as well as professionally, but whatever happened, my client was and still is committed to playing to her own true Intentions. She lives in the Picture of her life and the lives of her husband and their children moving forward. Her husband subsequently became a client of mine and now the whole family is thriving.

When we go to the symphony, the orchestra tunes to the musical note A as preparation for playing together in perfect harmony. There is a plethora of different sounds, but they all tune to play together in perfect pitch and harmony because they have been set to this one note. When we set the energy of the Heart, let's say to a note of A, we are setting up our space to invite the people around us to play with us in harmony.

Our Heart emanates waves of energy that move out like the waves of sound that comprise musical notes. These can be forceful waves, like those of a horn, or gentle waves, like those of a harp. Even though these different instruments are playing, they work together under agreement that they will stay in harmony.

Problems arise when another person doesn't choose to play in tune with the whole orchestra, but insists on playing according to their own out-of-tune vibration. If we go into agreement with that unharmonious tune, chaos is created. For example, when a spouse matches an off keynote that is being played by a partner who doesn't want to create harmony, then chaos in the person's life will ensue. Just like an orchestra avoids the cacophony of random sound, we need to agree to remain in tune and in harmony so that we can play in our lives. For instance, I have directed many of my clients with kids to download an app that makes a pitch perfect A sound, which they play when chaos with their kids begins to happen, so that they can bring themselves back to the present and not go into chaotic Pictures with their kids.

ENERGYWORKS METHOD

Tuning into the Vibration of the Heart

1. ***Tune to the note A by downloading a free tuning app so you can play it on your phone, or go on the Web so that you can hear and tune to the sound of A.*** This step sets you up to be in tune and to play and live your life in harmony with yourself and with others. Or, you can just hold the Intention of being in tune and harmony. Place your attention in your Heart. Imagine you are a tuning fork and tune your energy. Imagine the wave energy moving up and down in the vertical as a vertical wave, and imagine it moving out and back as a horizontal wave.

2. ***Set the color.*** Each color has a certain vibration, but the color you choose should be up to you. Once you've established this new wavelength that the color represents, everyone around you will start to match the vibration that you've set. You'll feel safe and secure within yourself because you won't get hammered by other people's negative wave patterns. You'll be creating the life you choose to live.

3. ***Set the wavelength.*** How do you want to move in your day? Do you want to be on a choppy wave or a smooth wave? Think about a trumpet versus a harp. Move your energy out like a wave in the ocean around the Earth. As this energy moves out, imagine people tuning into it and being in harmony.

4. ***Set the vibration.*** Determine the emotional tone—for example, peace, joy, or harmony—that you want to set in your space. How do you want to vibrate and move throughout your day? Play a song that

will put you in that vibration or mood. As this new energy comes into the Heart, feel the new vibration start to multiply and gain strength. Set the vibration and watch yourself move with the wave energy throughout your day. Let it carry you through all situations. You will flow from one situation to another.

Energy, from sound energy to light energy, moves in wave patterns, and each vibration has a different type of wave. Anger is a very choppy energy, and when someone vibrates anger, the wave that results begins to "unground" other energy around it. We are all conduits, and wave energy moves through us. Therefore, if we have not set our own vibrations, we will get swept away by the wave energy of others. When we walk into a room, it's external energy that we respond to. It is a matching game and whoever matches whom wins. If there is chaos and you match it, congratulations, you are good at matching and there will be chaos. If you can do that, then you can choose an energy that benefits everyone, including the angry person in the room. So, you need to be focused on your Heart energy and what wave you are running so that someone else will match your own energy, like love or joy.

There is also something like an undertow of energy that you can feel in your stomach and that is indeed wave energy that you are feeling, and that energy will pull you out to sea. Someone else is running energy and may be smiling, but you are feeling something else. That energy will start to live in you and become you, but if it does, say, "Match it, clear it," and then start to run your own Heart energy vertically up and down and then out and around.

When we set our Intention and own it, we will manifest it, but when a stronger wave vibration comes along, our Intention might collapse. The nature of a wave is that it goes up and down, and it has highs and lows. When we are on top of the wave, we are riding high, and when we are on the bottom of the wave, we're caught in the lows. Therefore, since energy moves in wave patterns, if we become caught in their currents, we find ourselves on an energy roller coaster. In physics, when a wave with the same amplitude and altitude hits another wave, the center will oscillate and cancel the wave. So, if you are holding onto one side of a jump rope and I am holding the other and we are moving it up and down on each side, at the same height and with the same motion, the center of that jump rope will not move. It will cancel the wave. That is what the Heart can do. So, when you feel something in your environment that causes you fear, worry, or anxiety, and you don't know what it is, but you feel it, tell the Heart, "Match that wave and cancel it," and it will do so outside of your space.

When we create our Intention, wave energy moves us to our ***Intention Space***. As the wave moves through these spaces, it shows us what we want and what we don't want. Like a coin, this Picture we're seeing has two different sides, but it is the same coin. If we get stuck on the Intention side and try to stay at the top of the wave, it will only drag us under, but if we experience the Intention and move it back to our Heart, we match the Intention as if we are living it. This is known as Being the Intention.

When we're caught in the negative, we can be sad and depressed, and our true Intention is buried. Have you heard people say, "I was doing so great and then everything fell apart"? That's simply the process of moving in a space that contains exterior information and vibration about what exists or doesn't exist. When we see one side as better than the other, we will always lose or win, experiencing both ups and downs. But if we open to the Wisdom of our Hearts, the Heart becomes the glue that brings opposite sides together to create a whole, and that's how we ride the wave. When we are whole, then we can create from the whole, and our Intention will reflect the whole.

When we master the energy that moves us and surrounds us, we inherit the Kingdom of Heaven on Earth by owning the throne of our Hearts.

Journaling

Draw a Heart in your journal. Write the word representing how you want to feel inside the Heart. Then choose a color and draw an ***Infinity Loop*** whose center is the center point of the Heart image. Trace that Infinity Loop multiple times just like an orchestra conductor would.

Body Movement

First, move one hand in an Infinity Loop like a conductor and feel the rhythm as you do so. You are setting, moving, and using your wave energy to activate your Intention, bringing it to life. You are commanding the energy to move, play, and be in harmony. Keep moving your hand. Then move both hands in a wave out and back in an Infinity Loop. When you move your hands, the energy in the space around you will start to move. If you are in a situation where the energy is chaotic, then you can move your hands in this Infinity Loop pattern.

8

Own Your Crown

If you don't own your crown, you're going down.

San Francisco has a famous annual celebration called Italian Heritage Day, and girls from around the area are sponsored by various local Italian clubs to compete for the title of Queen.

When I was nineteen years old, in preparation for the pageant, I imagined a Queen's crown on my head. I was painfully shy but had to speak in front of hundreds of people, so the image of wearing a crown and speaking to my assembled subjects helped me assume a royal command of the situation. At this point in my life, my creations were still based on hypnotherapy, sensory orientation, and having a written list of what I wanted. Dreaming and drifting were also a part of this process. My problem was that creating seemed to be hit or miss for me. Sometimes, I would be able to create my goal, but at other times I would create the opposite.

In any case, after being chosen as Queen, I created a list of attributes for the type of man that I'd like to date. He'd be Italian American and have green or dark eyes.

He'd be financially successful and creative, and he'd like to travel. I'm embarrassed to say that I had a punch list for what I wanted in a guy, but months later I was invited to a party and met someone who matched everything I'd written down. I'll call him JR. We talked for hours as the party went on around us, and we seemed to get lost in space and time while making an intense connection.

JR was a fashion designer. He had just won an award for designer of the year and his clothes were available in Barneys, Neiman Marcus, and all the other prestigious stores. The week after the party, he flew me to his home, and from that point on, I couldn't imagine being without him.

Within just a few months, JR proposed to me and presented me with a gorgeous diamond ring that his mother had left to him when she passed on. I've never seen anything so big on my finger. I was happy and in love, but when I came home to tell my parents about my engagement, no one seemed to be happy on my behalf. They didn't think I'd known JR long enough, and were thinking that I was attracted to his success. However, I'd had other boyfriends who had money and had never experienced a connection this strong, so I put my family's concerns aside.

Not long after our engagement, JR's father became seriously ill. This man had built a business empire from a corner fruit stand, a not unheard-of story among Italian immigrants in the first half of the twentieth century, and I loved him. My father-in-law-to-be was part of a network of local families who had risen to great heights in America but maintained a strong connection to their roots. I answered the phone at his house once and was speaking to Joe DiMaggio.

JR decided to put his design work on hold to run the family business. He moved back to San Francisco, and we moved in together. It was then that things started to fall apart. JR hurt his lower back and was in a lot of pain. We stopped sleeping together because he couldn't move in bed, and he subsequently became depressed because he wasn't creating his clothing line. The family business involved producing, and he was working market hours—getting up at two or three in the morning and going to bed by seven. I felt our relationship start to suffer. I blamed that on my own deficiencies, and because JR was going through a hard time in general, I committed to fixing myself and him.

JR was affectionate in public, and we seemed like the ideal romantic couple when we were out and about, but even after his back recovered, there was no physical connection. I felt like I was living with my brother, and I started to feel depressed myself. Every time I tried to get out of the relationship, though, he would pull me back in.

JR said things would change, but four years later nothing was different. His father's health was still declining, the demands of the business were ever present, and I felt that I was living the life of a nun. Then I stumbled across the list I'd made before we met. The one thing I didn't have on the list was a great physical connection. I'd never had that issue with anyone previously, so it hadn't occurred to me that a couple might live together without having sex.

JR continued to insist that we'd be together forever, but his actions expressed the opposite. He became controlling and bossy and narcissistic. He would scream and yell at me, and I'd believe that his anger and depression were my fault. It is easy to become stuck emotionally when your partner tells you what you want to hear, then does the opposite, and you try to heal it, fix it, and solve it. I was hanging onto the time when we first met, when our relationship was flowing and moving, and things simply worked. But the moment the relationship stopped working, I should've dropped it and left. The lesson I learned going through that situation was to let go. Energetically, when you try to fix someone and your energy runs in them and theirs runs in you, it will never resolve no matter what you do, and you will remain stuck and sick. You need to drop it and leave it. It is not your problem; that is the big lesson. This is why most people are stuck in unhappy relationships that they try to fix, solve, or resolve.

It took me several years to unravel and to build up my self-esteem enough to leave because JR had convinced me that I was at fault. I believed that something was wrong with me and that I needed to change. I eventually learned that by trying to fix myself and him as a way of trying to fix the relationship, nothing would ever improve. I realized that to change something, we must let it go. We must let it die and create something new.

My heart hurt so badly from this relationship that I had to heal it and open up to the wisdom within. This is the point when I started to really practice energy work and started to learn a new way of creating from the whole. Because I longed for what I'd lost, I started to move my attention inward, sending energy to my Heart, and my Heart began to heal.

As soon as I left JR, he found a new girlfriend, and I was devastated. I'd see them drive by and would think that if I had only been like her, things would have worked. She was a designer, she spoke Italian, and she seemed perfect in every way. Meanwhile, JR would still call me up when he had a problem or an anxiety attack because I was the only person who could calm him down. His new girlfriend actually liked this arrangement because it freed her from dealing with these situations, and when problems came up, she'd tell him to call me. I was still healing him and trying to heal the past relationship because I didn't know how to just end it.

I wish I had a dollar for every client who's come into my office telling me how wonderful the person they were in relationship with had been initially and how things had turned out to be the opposite. Sometime later, I got a phone call from that same girlfriend of JR's, asking me if I had experienced a lack of intimacy after my first year with him. She started telling me her story, and it sounded exactly like mine. I was heartbroken for her, but I felt relieved that it wasn't just me who had had the problem. After they split up, JR came back to me, professing his undying love and swearing that we could make it work. But he was a day late and a dollar short. I'd met someone else. Just recently, JR's other girlfriend recognized me in passing and stopped me to thank me for sharing my story with her and helping her to move on from JR. She told me that she had met the love of her life and had two wonderful children.

At this point, I had let go of the idea of upgrading my punch list as a means of trying to create what I wanted in a partner. I realized that I needed to create from the Heart and own my crown instead. I also noticed that when I focused only on reflective meditation, I wasn't focused on my Intention and goals. Not having that focus on Intention allowed me to be centered, but I never created anything. I discovered the balance of using what I'd learned earlier about creating an Intention and fueling it with Heart's energy to realize my goals. I became a student of observing the world around me and looking at Nature as a reflection of how energy moves within us. This was how I discovered many of the tools that I now use in my practice, and in particular, the importance of my crown.

Like a Ferris wheel, our emotions take us up and down and around and around. When we reach the top, if the view is clear, we can see for miles, and we feel as if there's nothing we can't do. When we rotate down, our feelings deflate. We feel that nothing can go right. But in order for energy to move, there needs to be a circuit. We need to unify the ups and downs to avoid being dizzy at the top and deflated at the bottom. We do this by centering our attention in the Heart and moving it up to the crown and back down.

I like to imagine that we each have a crown on our head like the crowns of royalty. That is where we have the ability to access our spiritual information. When we own our crown, we are remembering who we are as Spirit in a body, and we can live our life's purpose. Owning our crown is about owning what we create. When we own our crown, we have continuous insights, clarity, and access to our higher selves. We can align with our dreams and purpose and know who we are.

By owning our crown, we lead with the Spirit and the body follows. Like a queen or king sitting on a throne, we are seated at the highest point on the body and can see what's below us. We are gazing from our penthouse, which makes it easier for us to have perspective.

When we don't own our crown, we lose our connection to the universe and become entangled and stuck on the horizontal plane of the external world, in a swamp.

Our thoughts can be so strong that our mind will divide our energy, splitting it into duality. We tend to think that to be successful we have to be well connected to other people. But to advance, we need to be connected *up*, out of the mind and into our dreams.

The mind will dethrone you, depriving you of your crown and your ground and your connection to your higher purpose. It will also attach you to other people and to material objects. This is a process that takes place on the horizontal plane. The mind will also attach you to outside ideas, like the drive for power.

Most people are attached to someone or something, and their energy becomes entangled. They do, in fact, get energy by becoming entangled with others. This entanglement gives them energy to move, but this energy is limited; it's short-lived like the effects of a cup of coffee, and they crash once they run out of fuel. Then they find someone else to become entangled with for the next boost of energy they need to create. This is why people can't come up with original ideas, this is why they take from others, and this is why they lack autonomy and personal creativity.

When we connect to the people around us, we start to take on their energy, and they start to take on ours. Life is then full of entanglements and eventual disappointment. We may give to or take from others, but the energy usually tends to flow more strongly in either one direction or the other. For energy to really move, we need to have a circuit of requesting and receiving vertically up to Source and back down to the planet to create flow because the circuit is always moving in the vertical plane, but in the horizontal plane, you may receive or you may not. It is hit or miss. It doesn't always come back. But most people in the horizontal playing field don't have a circuit. Instead, they manipulate each other to control the energy between them as their own, and the result is either to someone's advantage or someone else's detriment. The ultimate result is gridlock.

When we are entangled with others and with the external world on the horizontal playing field, the ride we are on is like the teacups at Disneyland; we spin around and around in circles, never getting anywhere. We either spin out of control, burn out, or don't understand why we can't move forward. There is no focus nor direction. When we're not committed to connecting our energy upward to Source, we're living out another person's drama. We take on their baggage and the attachments that keep us stuck until we master this lesson.

Think of the crown like a launching pad for a rocket. It's where your Spiritual energy collects and is stored up above before it moves into your body. When you own your crown, you have the ability to connect up to the blueprint of your life's purpose.

The first part of creating what we want is dreaming, a manifestation of the nonphysical space. It gives us the means to imagine what doesn't exist. To create new possibilities through dreaming, we need to move up and out of our space and to discover new frontiers. The launching pad for this process is the crown. The crown connects us to our Spirit and our life's purpose.

Client Story

A second grade teacher came to see me, exhausted from dealing with a chaotic class that was out of control. She could neither get the kids to listen nor to focus their energy. At home, her husband was domineering and authoritarian, and she was constantly criticized for virtually everything that might go wrong. Even problems that didn't involve her were declared to be her fault. Her own two children were subjected to "walking on eggshells" because of their father's unpredictable and unstable behavior, so the environment she came home to was just as unsettling as the one at school. She came to me desperate to gain control of her life, as opposed to living in response to the chaotic energy that was being continually thrust at her.

The first tool I imparted to her was to own her crown. I had her imagine a crown on top of her head. This focused her attention on the place where her power resided so that she could have certainty and command the life she wanted to create, instead of getting her head cut off every day. I had her further imagine that she was a queen sitting on her throne, commanding the reality that she wanted in her kingdom. Without the notion of bossing people around, I had her imagine a classroom where the attention of the students was naturally directed toward learning and the enjoyment of learning, and where the "subjects" in her "kingdom" were happy to agree to this new state of being. In this way, she commanded her Pictures and ran her Heart Wave to set the space at joy so that she and her students could experience and move in that flow.

I also brought in an analogy based on my experience over the years with horses. To train a horse, the trainer has to get the horse's energy moving in a circuit. The trainer occupies the center of the training ring in a vertical position, owning their crown and being connected and moving energy up and down, while the horse circles the perimeter of the ring on the horizontal.

I had my client imagine that, when in the center of her classroom, she was in the center of a riding ring with a crown on her head. The goal of the horse trainer is to get the horse to move in an orderly motion in a circuit. When the horse and trainer are in agreement, with the trainer in command, there is movement with purpose and intent. I gave my client that image to work with so that she could direct the energy of the class in a circuit. This image activated the energy to create harmony and an atmosphere of learning with enthusiasm. She also presented the class with a series of mental Pictures (a much more effective approach), as opposed to a series of verbal commands, and a new reality was activated. The attention of the class was captured in a profound and wonderful way as they moved their energy through these Pictures, and she's a happy and highly regarded teacher today.

Owning her crown at home, my client found that she was not in a relationship, but in fact was living under her husband's dictatorship, a situation that, up to then, she had responded to by cooperating. Having gotten out of agreement with that state of affairs, she is now creating a life for herself and her children based on harmony and support. Her husband was unable and unwilling to be part of that, and they are getting divorced. My client is now bringing in a new reality and letting go of something that didn't serve her true purpose. She's got peace in her kingdom and ownership of her crown.

ENERGYWORKS METHOD

Owning Your Crown and Moving Upward to Connect with Your Dreams

1. ***Imagine a crown on the top of your head.*** By placing your attention on top of your head, you will be able to access your Spiritual reservoir. The Spirit comes through the crown, and that is where information is stored. When you own your crown, you remember what you came here to do as a Spirit in the body. And even if you can't remember, just by placing your attention there, it will start to activate, and you will start to own your energy and information in the body. You will then be able to command things to happen. This is also known as the space of no effort. This is where you imagine, and things manifest into being. No effort is involved because you have stepped out of your old Pictures to command the new Picture and new vibration you want to see and feel. It is not in the how; it is in the now. This is where you can have it. Owning your crown is establishing your connection with the Unified Field. And this determines what you are connected to. So, to create beyond what you know, you must be connected to the Creator. This is your most important connection. And this way, whatever you are connected to is what you are filled up with, so if you are connected to the Unified Field, you will be filled with Spirit and Light. You have access to all your power. This is the place of accessing your imagination and your dreams and co-creating with Spirit. It is the launching pad to go up and create beyond what you know.

2. ***Create a circuit of relationship to the Unified Field of Request and Receive and launch your Intentions.*** First, you established a connection to the Unified Field. Now, you are establishing communication with the Field. In this communication, there is a co-creation. So, connecting from the Heart to the Unified Field creates in a circuit, and the circuit is the movement of energy. This is where you Request, and this is where you Receive because this is the circuit of relationship. Place your order!

3. ***Move your Heart Wave up and down to create your dreams.*** Moving your Heart Wave up into the abstract or into no form—otherwise known as the unknown or the pure energy of God—is the Request. The Heart shoots the Intention, or Request, like a rocket, way up to the edge of the Universe, creating space. This is where you don't have to be attached to it and can let it go. This is the first part of creation. In Receiving, the energy lowers and drops down, moving into form, which you Receive in the physical body. This is where the Unified Field will respond to your Request. It hasn't yet, but it will, and will give you feedback as to your next steps in so doing.

4. ***Receive your Intention.*** The Heart is the bridge between the Spirit and the body. It's the place where things enter and become integrated and whole. When you open to the Wisdom of the Heart, you create a circuit of Request and Receive from your Heart up to the Unified Field and back to your Heart. This is the intimate relationship between you and the Unified Field. Hand over your energy, ask the Unified Field to co-create with you, and see

what comes back. The moment you let go of your Intention, it will disassemble and reassemble into a new form. This is how we co-create with the Unified Field. It's this circuit of connection, communication, and co-creation that builds a relationship with the Unknown and allows you to be in a creative process. However, you must open your Heart up to Receive. Your response creates your reality. You must respond. A block or Backspace Picture may show up in your world. If you respond to it as if it were real, you have not learned your lesson. Whatever is showing up needs releasing, so you must let it go. You must remain neutral no matter what. You take the position of the crown. You remain calm and collected like a queen.

5. ***If you get stuck, liquify your thoughts in a blender in your mind's eye so that you have no thoughts.*** If you start to think, you will get stuck, meaning that you have gone into your mind and not into your Heart. When you are in your Heart, it moves like a Ferris wheel, up and down and around. You have to hand over your Intention to God and let it go.

The crown reminds us of our higher selves in every situation. If we move upward and co-create with the Unified Field, we'll have greater awareness, gain greater perspective, and achieve more insights (because of our connection to God), all of which we can then bring back into the body. The crown is the highest point. It's like the penthouse at the top of an apartment building. You have a view of the whole landscape before you because you are on top of the mountain.

Rising from the base of the spine upward through the central channel takes a lot of energy. But to avoid a long, slow journey, we need the Heart, with all of its spontaneous energy, to blast off. Once we make it out of the atmosphere, we start to float and dream in space. Our dreams get reflected back to us from the stars, like a mirror reflecting our Intention throughout the network of the Universe. We can imagine communication coming back to us from all the stars in the field as we state our Intention, moving back down into the atmosphere through our crown and then through our Heart and into our body.

Our goal upon reentering the atmosphere is not to forget who we are and how we are connected. The crown is the place of entry—a tool to help us remember our purpose and to unify our Intention before bringing it into the body, allowing us to truly live.

The crown represents our ability to command and control the energy coming in and out of the body. When we own this space, we will have an ability to see our dreams and perceive whether they're aligned with our higher purpose. We will also have the determination to confront any challenge and change it. When we own our crown, people recognize who we are, they see us, and we are validated. We won't allow people to project Pictures on us, and we won't play out the distorted dramas that they possess and try to share. Owning our crown is about owning our birthright and the ability to imagine and manifest what we came here to do.

When we're a king or queen, we have a cause and a purpose. We own our kingdom, and we control the energies that are manifested in our space.

Journaling

Identify your Intention and write it down. In your journal write, "Source, I am requesting (*put in your order like you are ordering food, which actually represents your Intention*) or something greater." Then write, "I am Receiving (*your Intention*)."

Body Movement

Write down your Intention or imagine it in an object. Either crumple up the paper, or take the object (preferably a ball) and throw it in the air, saying out loud, "I Request. I Receive." Another body movement is to wear or draw a crown. Or, make one from natural elements out in Nature. If you are drawing or painting one, make sure to include lots of colorful gems or all diamonds, if you prefer, to remind you that you come from the stars and you are a Diamond body of light. Then imagine or say out loud, "I Request. I Receive."

9

Own Your Ground

After I broke up with JR, I saw a handsome man at a party and approached him. Peter was a few years younger than me, a philosophy and environmental student at Berkeley, and he was passionate and connected to the natural world.

I spent a couple of years with Peter. I had been working obsessively, and his low-key, kicked-back approach to life provided a useful example for me, in that although he had no fortune, he supported himself comfortably as a painter of fancy Victorian houses. His connection to the natural world seemed to facilitate his ability to flow through life, and I learned to relax during our time together. His energy was like a walk through the forest.

Peter and I went camping and on trekking trips that cost us very little but that had infinite value in my life. When we were trekking, Peter and I slept under the stars for days at a time, and I connected with Nature in a profound way. The experience transformed me, but Peter, over time, became critical, judgmental, and eventually unfaithful. One day, after walking away from Peter to escape his criticism, I found myself looking down on him from a promontory, high above a beach where he was sitting. Gazing out at the ocean, I felt connected in a completely new way. While looking back down at Peter, however, I felt isolated and inadequate. I've since come to realize that the relationship we have with people can be isolating and disconnected, but that nature is a true and constant source of wholeness. In that crucial moment up on the cliff, I chose the ocean. I was able to let go of Peter, but the connection to the planet that I developed during my time with him solidified my self-esteem and led me to the love of my life.

I was in the gym working out one day, not long after, when I said hello, in passing, to a dark-haired man with green eyes. This guy was gorgeous, and my first thought was that he must have lots of women, so I kept myself from being interested. I later learned that he'd gone home that night and told his mother he'd seen the woman he was going to marry. She asked him the girl's name and he said, "I don't know." She then asked, "Did you talk to her?" He said, "No."

He soon asked me out to dinner. I was very attracted to him, but I was still on the rebound from Peter. My focus at that time had turned inward. I had decided to pursue a master's degree and was focusing on my Heart. But, interestingly, when I focused within, it seemed to cause change in the world around me, and creating became much easier. On our third date, he took me to see a Broadway show, and on the way home I said, "You know, you should probably get a new car."

He replied, "I love this car. I take great care of it, and I've had it for years." Then the next day he called me up, sounding strange. He said he'd been driving home from work and his car had died on the Golden Gate Bridge. It was towed to a mechanic who told him that the cost of repairing it would be more than the car was worth.

My new love interest asked me how I knew something was wrong with his car. In fact, he asked me if I was a witch. But the simple fact is that, although the car looked terrific, it had spoken to me. This isn't as crazy as it sounds. A real part of my Native American heritage is an affinity for connecting, communicating, and being in relationship with the natural world. Although the car was an object, like all objects it had a frequency of its own and a connection to Nature. I could tell that the frequency was off. My senses in this regard were especially acute because I had recently been spending time in the wilderness.

From our first real conversation, this new man in my life told me that he wasn't good in relationships, and I responded, "Yeah, I can see that you are attracted to really crazy energy, and I'm not that." I then confirmed that it would be better for him to not be in relationship. We built our connection from there. After six months, we moved in together and things got comfortable, but I was afraid he'd never ask me to marry him. So, I went away to Canada to visit family for two months with the Intention that when I got back either he'd propose or we'd be done.

Upon my return, he asked me to drive up to Eugene, Oregon, his family's hometown. He took me to a butte overlooking a spectacular view and was about to speak when a bad smell hit us. We realized we were next to a porta-potty. We moved a few feet away, where he handed me a ring from a Cracker Jack box and proposed. It wasn't the most romantic of beginnings, but it exemplified my husband's basic down-to-earth nature. That moment by the porta-potty became the ground and Foundation upon which we built our happy life together.

Your "ground" is the Foundation upon which everything is built. Nature is God in a form that reflects your own nature. To understand yourself, you have to have a relationship with Nature to discover and understand your own nature. It is where physical information for the body is stored. This Foundation stores the energy and information from our family tribe. Even if we don't know who our parents are, their energy and information are in our Foundation. We are born into a vibration, which encompasses our values, customs, and beliefs, and which constitutes our family agreement. These are the hardest agreements to break because they are at our root and because they are the field we originally learn to play on.

When we're children, we don't question our playing field. We may not like it, but we don't have the information to create something new. However, there's a time in all of our lives when many of us realize that we're on shaky ground. It's a point in our process when we must break from the family tribe, pull up our roots, and build a Foundation of our own. It was extremely difficult for me to break from my tribe to go to college, to have a strong healthy body, to feel secure, to not be overtaken, and to thrive financially. These were all things that were not a part of my family agreement but that I had to create on my own. I had to go back all the way to my childhood at the dump to find new ground to stand on so that what I built would grow and thrive.

When we own our ground, we're remembering where we came from, as well as our ancestors who affect us. We're grateful for the lessons learned on that playing field. We forgive our family and our tribe for playing out the genetic line and the energetic patterns that have been passed down over the years. Every year the outermost ring of the redwood tree dies and becomes the skeleton on which the new Foundation is formed. If you cut a redwood tree in half, you can see what happened in time and the redwood tree's history—when there was a drought, when there was a fire. But, all in all, the redwood tree learned to survive. So, we must first understand that what we think are our issues are not always the case.

When we're aware, we can let go of the old Foundation and create a new one that is based on awareness and wisdom—one that is solidly grounded in what we want to create in our body and in life. When we own our ground, we take a stand for what we want to build as our life's purpose. Owning our ground is about owning the Foundation we create on, and then owning what gets built. It's about having our actions, thoughts, and feelings match our energy vibration. When we own our ground, we own the land we stand on. Owning it gives us the ability to create in the physical world.

By owning our ground, we take a stand for the body and its right to physically thrive and be here. Even though we all have bodies, often our energy doesn't fully occupy the body and its Foundation, and this affects what we can create on the physical plane. When we are entirely in the body, we claim our birthright to the Earth as our home, and we commit to being here. When we stand our ground and make this commitment, we say yes to our life, and we move in the world in a new way.

When we don't own our ground, we lose our connection to the Earth, and we become rooted to the horizontal world. But trees don't grow sideways and neither do we. When we root to others, our roots give those people our energy. And if we try to build off others first, instead of from the ground, we'll be disappointed; our roots won't grow since the energy of others won't work in us. God's energy works in us, but any other energy doesn't work. We tend to think that to be successful we have to be grounded to other people. But to grow, we need to be grounded down to the Earth, just like a tree, which lifts up its branches to the sun, or God's energy.

Our roots want to attach to objects or other people, looking for a Foundation. But when we root to someone or something else, our roots become so entangled that we don't have the ability to move, and ultimately our growth is stunted. We may have our roots connected to more than one person or thing. If we have no space for our roots to grow, we will continue to find new people or objects to send our roots to, or they will find us. Redwoods, as tall and mighty as they are, do not have deep roots, but they do have lots of padding that protect them from not absorbing the energy of others. They have the most efficient circulation system from the roots to the tips of their branches, and if you tie something around the trunk of a redwood tree, like a hammock, you will kill the tree. The heart of a redwood tree, like the heart of humans, is a circulation system that circulates energy. That's why if you focus on the Heart, energy will move. But if you focus on the mind, you will live in duality, and your energy will become stuck. It will not come back, which is why you become anxious. *You know you are stuck in the mind if you are thinking about the future or if you're living in the past or if you see the world as half empty or full. In other words, you can see the world from only one side: as positive or negative. The Heart, however, does not see that way.*

For this reason, many people attach to objects or other people as their Foundation. Suffering is caused by this kind of attachment, and when our roots attach to someone or something, we resist letting go. We need something to root to be able to grow, but the only way our roots can thrive is by grounding to our true home, and that is the Earth.

Client Story

My client, a woman in her mid-forties, had issues with men. She would shut down when in their presence because she did not know how to respond to their conversations. Sometime after our work together had begun, my client went home for the holidays, where she shared a story over dinner with her family about a sex-discrimination trial that had taken place in our community. Her father, out of the clear blue, became angry and yelled at her, "Why are we even talking about this?" It was a spontaneous outburst designed to shut my client down. She immediately moved inward in response and felt her Heart closing down. She shrank and lost her voice, not knowing what to say. There was dead silence in the room; no one in her family had a way to address the father's venom. This incident brought her back to her family roots and the way her father had set the space for all of them and maintained control over the years. It was this root that created her issues as an adult with men in general, basically a regular feeling of being attacked and collapsing inwardly. More damaging was her tendency, in the face of this attack energy, to then blame and attack herself.

My client and I had spent our sessions working on owning her ground. When this latest incident occurred, after the initial shock but very much in the same moment, she put her attention on her Heart and being grounded to the Earth and started to release her father's dominating energy out of the family gathering. Her attention had at first moved to the window in an attempt to escape because she was dissociating, but she was determined to let go of her old roots, ground the body, release the pain, and allow the planet to renew the space. The silence at the table persisted, until her sister suddenly stood up and spoke for her—something that had never happened before—and said, emphatically, "Let her finish."

The father got up at that point and left the room, but the family pulled out the game Monopoly, proceeded to play, and had a great time for the rest of the evening. For the first time in years of these family games, my client wound up owning hotels on Boardwalk. The father came back in eventually and joined the fun, something that in the past he had routinely found a way to ruin.

For my client, the success of the whole episode was clearly seeing the root of her inability to maintain her space with men in general and then to be able to renew that part of her life. Now she feels grounded, rooted, and safe in the same situations that formerly caused her to collapse and lose her voice. She speaks up, is no longer attacked, and moves her energy down into the ground.

ENERGYWORKS METHOD

1. ***Imagine the base of your spine and imagine a grounding rod or tree to the center of the Earth.*** To create something new, you cannot rely on your old Foundation. You must first face and own the Foundation you were born on so that you can change it and create something new. You must let go

of your old roots to create new ones. It is important to break from the tribe and have your own roots because doing so ensures survival. To do that, you must ground and release. When you ground, you are getting rid of the energy that you have absorbed or taken on that is not yours, like emptying a bathtub of dirty water, so that you can be open to receiving the light and the energy of your crown down to your ground. When you are grounded, you are safe, secure, stable, and supported.

2. ***Create a circuit of relationship from your Heart to the Earth of Release and Renew, and let go of what you don't want.*** By letting go of what you don't want, you are letting go of the energy that you have absorbed that is not yours or any negativity, fear, or anxiety. By grounding, you are able to release. Grounding allows you to be safe, secure, stable, and supported. So, if a negative person is around you, you won't become affected by that energy. You can ground it out and Release it and let it go, just like every home that has a lightning or grounding rod. If lightning strikes your house, that energy will take the path of least resistance and your house will not catch fire because your outlets are grounded. So, grounding is letting go of the discharge so that you don't become it, play it out, or live it. You drop down and ground. If someone blasts you and you start to react, you become it because you're in it and you identify it as yours, but it's not. All you need to do is let go of it. Don't resist it, and it will move through you and ground out of you. You will feel it, but if you ground it down and just let

go, you will be in the flow. Say to yourself, "Ground down; let it go. I am in the flow. I am safe, secure, stable, and supported."

3. ***Move your Heart Wave down and up to create your dreams.*** From your Heart, move your energy down to the planet to communicate, "I am releasing what I don't want to you, Planet, so you can recycle it and I can Renew my body with new energy and information to grow and thrive." By doing this, you are asking the planet for an update and Renewal.

4. ***Let the body Renew.*** Because the Heart is in relationship with the planet and you are letting go of what you don't want, you are asking the planet to allow the seeds of your Intention that you have planted to grow upward. When you focus on your Heart, the update from Earth moves through your body so that your Intention can manifest in the body. The blueprint of creation starts with the Intention within your Heart. Then you ask the Unified Field what it thinks, and you hand it over. You open your Heart to Receive. You must then create space by Releasing whatever is in you that doesn't match this new reality. And then you focus on the Heart and a Renewal happens in you. The body starts to Renew with current information. This is the cycle of creation. And it will be your next evolutionary jump. This is the Heart's journey, which goes around and around in relationship with the planet and the Unified Field/Source, and each time you change and transform.

Journaling

Write down your Intention on paper, as if it were a seed. Rip the paper off the pad and bury it outside in the dirt or imagine yourself doing so, saying, "I'm Releasing this into the ground, and I'm Renewing with the growth of my Intention."

Body Movement

Take a ball and bounce it on the floor. Move it down and up, or just run a circle down and around, saying, "I am grounding my Intention. I am Renewing my Intention."

10

Intention

Intense shyness remained a serious problem for me as I entered high school. Over a thousand students were enrolled in each grade, and I had but a single friend when I started, a girl named Becky, whom I'd known since middle school. Furthermore, because the school had a multiracial population in an era of racial tension, there was a lot of conflict. Gang fights were common, and people died.

My brother, who was a stoner in high school, would drive me to school every morning while smoking a joint. We didn't have a defroster in the car, so he'd continually have to wipe the windshield to see where he was going, while blowing out smoke that filled the car, like a Cheech and Chong movie. Along the way we'd pass the steps of the public library, where two of the local gangs hung out. Both gangs were white supremacist groups. All the guys were out of school, but they used the high school as a recruiting ground.

From the very beginning of high school, I remember that the other girls didn't like me. To make matters worse, I was asked out that year by a boy from a Mexican gang in another town, and I eventually attended the prom with him. My dating him made me a target for the white supremacist gang and their girlfriends. I had no idea at the time that going out with a Mexican boy, especially to the prom, would land me on a hit list. Girls came up to me, pushed me around, and said they were going to kick my ass. Even Becky, my best friend, approached me in front of a gang of girls and pushed me to the ground. I was wearing a pair of earrings that she'd lent me, but she proclaimed out loud that I'd stolen them and demanded them back. Devastated and uncomprehending, I left school early and cried for hours. I was now isolated and alone, with no friends whatsoever. For the rest of my freshman year, the school security guards would walk me to class to keep me from getting beaten up. These girls were tough. They fought physically and constantly. My former friend, Becky, actually broke a boy's jaw. I was terrified to the point of contemplating suicide.

I was at home one day, in the midst of all this, when my father grabbed me and took me down to the local Denny's. On the boys' bathroom wall, someone had written, "Kim Carbone is a slut." He was furious. (I hadn't even had sex yet.) The only boy I'd dated was the one who'd taken me to the prom. This message was someone's revenge for my having dared to go out with a Mexican boy.

Finally, by the beginning of tenth grade, I managed to move beyond the nightmare scenario of the previous year. At the end of ninth grade, I had met a girl named Lynn, who was really smart and an outstanding student. Ironically, since I was so insecure about my learning issues, we related to each other as fellow oddballs, albeit different types. Lynn was interested in reading, writing, and poetry, and my friendship with her began to open up those worlds for me. She also had dated the head of the white supremacist gang and was able to intercede for me to have the pressure taken off. We both joined the track team and started to encourage and support each other, and we became inseparable. I was devastated when she became a foreign exchange student and went to Japan, leaving me alone once more. But I was used to being isolated, and thanks to her influence, I decided to focus on school and to try to learn.

At that time, I also became interested in modeling, and I entered a competition. I used the self-hypnosis that my Aunt Lillian had taught me for years to put myself in a state of already having won, and lo and behold, I did win.

This was my use of the abracadabra system of speaking my words into creation. The self-hypnosis technique consisted of simply reading aloud statements about what I wanted to achieve, but I added visualization of what it would feel like, what it would taste like, and even what it would smell like to win. I used the senses in this way to anchor myself in the moment of winning. This bit of success gave my self-confidence an important boost.

Back at school, I became attracted to the foreign exchange students, the nerds, and anyone else who was left out of the crowd. We could identify with each other because we felt like outsiders, but by the twelfth grade, in spite of myself, I became popular. Part of that was the result of being independent and learning to stand on my own.

However, one foreign exchange student, an Italian boy named Tino, persisted that year in being mean to me. During the last two weeks of school, I started to talk to him, and sure enough, we fell in love.

Then Tino's cousin, an exchange student in Texas, came to visit. The most popular cheerleader in the school, a girl who hadn't talked to me in four years, suddenly became friendly because she wanted to date this guy, and for those last two weeks, the four of us were constantly together. We realized what a loss it had been not to have known each other throughout high school and learned an important lesson about prejudice.

High school finally ended, and everyone who hadn't dropped out or died from the old gangs graduated. Tino had to return to Italy, but he gave me a ring, declared his undying love, and promised me we'd stay connected. The Mexican boy I'd dated in the ninth grade had been killed in a gang fight by then, and another friend had died by suicide. Many of my former classmates had become hardcore drug addicts, and others were already in prison. The nerds, cheerleaders, and drama kids went on to college.

I'd never thought about going to college, since my parents had never talked about it. But I'd taken Tino seriously, and my heart was set on Italy. Going there was all I could think of, and the walls of my room became covered with posters of every part of that country. I listened to Italian music, and day in and day out, I visualized being there. I visualized the smells and tastes, using all of my senses to immerse myself in this Picture. I used Italian language tapes to speak the language, and that made the experience very real. It was a process that grew out of my success in modeling.

One thing I knew I needed before I could realize any kind of dream at this stage was money. I had been teaching aerobics to earn a little money during high school, and I read that a local Jane Fonda aerobics studio was holding auditions. I tried out with thousands of other people, and incredibly, I was taken aside and told that I'd be a natural for teaching aerobics in Italy. I was referred to and interviewed by an Italian fitness company, and they hired me, bought me a plane ticket, and sent me on my way. Here, out of the clear blue, was my first experience of creating a reality beyond the one that I currently occupied.

While on the plane, I met an Italian shoe salesman, who taught me a new word, *scarpe,* which means shoes. Ironically, he wore red shoes like Dorothy in *The Wizard of Oz*. Scarpe and shoes are both symbols of Foundation, and here I was, getting off the plane, ready to start my new life on a new Foundation. So, as my feet landed on Italian soil, I clicked my heels three times, like Dorothy had done, and said out loud, "I now have a successful career in Italy—Abracadabra."

Within a short time of arriving in Milan, I began sharing an apartment with a fellow instructor and teaching aerobics. We were the first aerobics instructors in the city, and soon we had seven different locations and a local TV show.

My goal in doing all of this was to hook up with Tino. I finally joined him for a family vacation, but wound up spending more time learning to ski with his father than I did reconnecting with him, and our relationship ended. That was a rough blow, but I moved on.

My method for learning the Italian language consisted of sitting in the local cafes and listening. Near my apartment, there was a newsstand run by an elderly man who spoke no English, but he befriended me. Every morning I visited him, and he would speak and read to me. At night I would listen to the radio and try to "feel" the Italian language by feeling its vibration. I put myself in the position of a toddler learning language from the ground up, and gradually I became fluent, so much so that I started to teach aerobics on television.

The company that had brought me to Italy folded, but I landed a job teaching aerobics on a Russian cruise ship that traveled around the Adriatic. On board, I met an Italian film producer who invited me to stay at his castle-like home in the middle of Rome, but my time with him was short-lived because he had a cocaine habit, like Scarface. Unlike scarpe, that was something I wanted no part of; that was no Foundation for me. One little adventure followed another, including living on a park bench, but I saved my pennies along the way until I finally had enough money to go home. I left Italy and, with command of a new language and some knowledge of the broader world, I returned to northern California.

The Italian experience had been romantic and exciting, even when things hadn't gone well, and being back where I'd started now seemed depressing. But I was nineteen years old and had to find a job right away, so I started to create Pictures of a new and exciting life in California, specifically one that included travel. I landed a survival-type position at a chiropractic office as a receptionist, and my boss invited me to go with him to a seminar.

The company giving the seminar had a nationwide business teaching patient education, and during the weekend I became friendly with the owner. He wound up offering me an opportunity to move to Los Angeles and help him put on seminars across the country. This opportunity sounded too exciting to pass up, so I grabbed it.

The job was in Westwood, near UCLA. My boss and I got off to a rocky start because it was very clear that I didn't have an advanced education. In fact, I didn't even know how to write out a check. But the new boss persevered with me, and I was sent to a Xerox training course on selling. There, I was given tools that, along with the basic points of selling, consisted of creating a space, or "bubble," and imagining that space as a place where I could communicate. It was a technique I could relate to, so I mastered it. I called up doctors across the country and sold them our seminars.

In this position, I'd found something that I was really good at. I noticed that on the phone I could build relationships with people that in some ways seemed more intimate than those I might establish in person. Even if I didn't sell a seminar, we'd have a stimulating conversation, and that became something I thrived on. I made my boss a lot of money. Every weekend we would travel, and I would set up the seminars and support him while he made his presentations. Yet even though at nineteen I was making good money, I knew that I had to go back to school to get a basic foundation for the future. That's when I went to college, got sick, recovered, and founded Timesavers. My next step was a master's degree, the place from which my understanding of "Intention" finally took off.

I was still in the process of getting my master's degree at the University of San Francisco when I met my future husband. We met, fell in love, and got married over a period of about a year. My husband had a sales job at the time and was making a transition into real estate, and even though my degree was in Life Transition Counseling, he wanted me to join him in his new business. I bought into that, matched his Picture as it were, and began to scout leads and solicit clients. My experience with Timesavers played a big role in this. Through Timesavers, still being managed by my mom, I knew people who were buying and selling homes. I was extremely successful and was even being consulted on a fee basis by other Realtors, strictly to take advantage of my command of space and energy to sell homes. I generated virtually all of my husband's business and got to the point where I decided to obtain a real estate license of my own.

Two things happened to alter this direction: I couldn't pass the real estate exam, and my relationship with my husband began to blow up. He became competitive and resentful of my success, and he stopped following up on new business. The stress this put on our marriage was enormous.

My learning disability was one cause of my five-time failure to pass the real estate exam, but the real issue was the fact that from the get-go, this phase of my life was being directed by other people's energy. I was operating on my husband's frequency and not my own.

I was barefoot and pregnant in the kitchen one day, cooking a big Italian dinner, when I suddenly woke up. I realized I was living life through my husband's Pictures of what he wanted me to be, working and making money, but still maintaining the role of a traditional housewife. I made a commitment in that moment to own my life and to pursue the work that I was born for. My husband worked in the local office of a large real estate firm. At the office Christmas party that year, I offered fifteen minutes of free sessions in a private room to everyone in attendance as a holiday gift, and they all took me up on it. The sessions consisted of my asking people what they wanted, helping them clear whatever blocks I could observe, and showing them a new field to play on that might move them toward their Intention to manifest their dream. My initial client list as a transformational life coach grew out of that evening.

Intention consists of bringing our awareness, attention, intention, and focused energy toward the horizon of what we want to create. It's not about attaching to a goal. It's about moving toward a target, what I call "Playing to your Picture." From where you sit is where you create. Isn't it interesting that the word *abracadabra* that we all used as children when we put on magic shows in our backyard is derived from the Hebrew words *ab* (the father), *ben* (the son), and *ruach hakodesh* (or holy spirit), or from the Aramaic *avra kadavra*, meaning "it will be created in my words."

In the previous chapter, you learned how to place your order with God by requesting what you want. Now, you'll learn about the power of your words in creating your Intention. Like a pilot in the cockpit of an airplane, we need to train ourselves to stay focused on the horizon to maintain our true direction.

Client Story

A female client was a retired professional race car driver. She came to me with a lot of different issues, not the least of which was her lack of direction and purpose following the end of her racing career. This situation was made worse by her feeling of having failed to achieve the highest level of her sport. Here was a woman who had defied the odds by establishing a viable racing career while working as a waitress and who had persevered in a male-dominated environment. She didn't let anyone else's Pictures of her deter her from her goal. Nevertheless, in the aftermath of all this, she was disregarding her significant accomplishments because she hadn't reached the Intention that she'd set up for herself. She was a national champion at her own level of the sport but had wanted to ultimately move up to Formula One—the major leagues, as it were—and that didn't happen.

My client's racing career ended when her sponsor was acquired by another company, and their racing program ended. Because her future husband had actively supported her dream of racing, at that time she made a decision to put her own passion aside and support him, to the exclusion of all else. She began raising a family and put her complete attention on them. Doing so led to a state of being scattered and anxious with regard to what she really wanted. Her husband had never insisted on this, but she took it upon herself to focus her attention on everyone but herself. She came to me on another client's recommendation, because her husband's business, where she now works, was struggling and she was also struggling with family issues.

I had my client observe where she sat with regard to her current life, and it was obvious that she was doing what she thought she had to do but was really sitting outside of her space. It was as if she was watching race cars go around a track, when she was meant to be in the race, behind the wheel. I had her pull her attention back into her cockpit, the center of her head, putting her into a state of pure being. From this place, she was able to understand that she needed to be living her own life and be focused on her own true Intention.

As she began to practice, a new business opportunity came into my client's life. She had adopted a means of using the skills that she acquired over years of training. As a driver, she had to keep her attention in the cockpit, or the center of her head, while keeping her body relaxed and her heart rate down. This technique allowed her to focus on the horizon at all times so that she could flow through the field and not crash, and she started to apply that to life as a whole. Because she was operating through second nature and without conscious, distracting thought, she was able to steer a true course. The fact that she had this remarkable ability as a result of the dream she had pursued put her back in the race. Now she feels calm, peaceful, happy, and alive.

Most people create their Intention outside of their space. They want to be somewhere other than where they are. The discrepancy between their body being in one place and their energy and attention being somewhere else stifles their movement, and they can't create. It's like driving into a blind fog and losing direction. For example, your breath is one thing; it has an inhale and an exhale. However, if you separate the two actions, your breath is no longer unified; it is, instead, divided into duality. Unconscious energy then occupies the space, and that is the block most people find themselves up against.

Do you observe your mind wandering around as if on a winding road, moving right, moving left? When you follow your attention, you create from what you want and from what you don't want, from the good and from the bad. But we are looking not to sit on one side or the other, on the positive or negative. We are looking to stay focused on our destination by sitting and occupying the cockpit in the center of our head, which will unify the two.

ENERGYWORKS METHOD

1. ***Own the center of your head.*** Imagine yourself as a race car driver, sitting in your cockpit, the center of your head, the location of the pineal gland. The pineal gland is a small, pinecone-shaped endocrine gland that sits in the center of the brain and produces melatonin, a serotonin-derived hormone that affects the modulation of sleep patterns in both seasonal and circadian rhythms. It thus controls the dream space where everything gets created and where all problems can be resolved. Being able to occupy that space of the pineal gland, which we can visualize as the cockpit in the center of the brain, enables us to see our Intention from our higher self. If we can occupy that space and see from our higher self, we can create from there as well. If you are traveling 200 miles an hour, you have no time for random thought or for your attention to wander. Your attention has to be centered in the cockpit and focused on the horizon so that you're able to be in the moment; otherwise, the car will crash.

2. ***Focus on the horizon.*** To concentrate on your Intention, focus your vision until you're looking outward from an imaginary third eye in the center of your forehead, a place where you can see yourself with no blind spot. The third eye is the windshield that looks out from the central space or cockpit. This eye gives you your view of the horizon and keeps you on the path to your destination. With all of your attention, with all of your energy, you must focus the mind's eye straight ahead to the horizon. When you are focused on the horizon, you are no

longer on a winding road; you're driving straight ahead. Imagine looking into the far horizon and seeing a mirage. Heat coming from the stars above hits the Earth, reflecting light onto the horizon, which looks like a sparkling Diamond. Keep your eyes fixed on this point. It's the point where the Intention comes through and then manifests into reality.

3. ***Create your Intention from your higher self.*** I want you to be driving to your Intention in a Formula One race car that will crash if you become distracted. This will force you to be fully present and aware in each moment and will get you to move toward your Intention. Many people lose their space if they are not able to achieve their Intention. If their goal is to win that race and they fail, they simply stop moving. But the more you move on the track to your Intention, the more precise you'll become. The more you ask your higher self to move your body on your path, the more alive you'll feel. You are present; you are able to see reality from the whole.

4. ***Access your dream and live it.*** Conclude your evening with this visualization every night before sleep. Ask your higher self and the Unified Field to resolve any problems you have and to help you create your Intention. Send it out to the stars. It's not important to remember your dreams. Then, every morning, ask to receive the download and information that comes back, saying out loud, "Let my Spirit lead me on the path of my Intention, and let my body follow." As we master this process, it is important

to understand that often our attention goes to other people because their energy comes at us, and this gives us a boost. But I want your Heart to be the fuel that powers the vehicle that drives you to your Intention. The Heart will fuel the mind to keep it focused so that you are locked on the Intention of your goal. When we focus our Intention while sitting in the cockpit of our race car, we can move through our life as intended. We won't swerve off onto any dead-end roads, and the things that come at us and distract us will bounce off the windshield as we continue to move through space. Directing our attention and where it goes determines what we create. From where we sit is where we create. When we sit in the center of our head, we set ourselves up to see from our higher selves (Spirit) and access our dream space, which is where all things are created. Then we can move through the day, viewing the horizon and enjoying the ride.

Journaling

Draw a Diamond. Fill it in with a color of your choosing. Gaze at it as you would a mirage, and imagine that you are driving toward this, your Intention. Throughout the day, keep that Diamond out in front of you between you and other people. Focus on your destination.

Body Movement

Get in a car (or imagine one if you don't have one) and place a Diamond on the front grill (or in your head) and imagine being driven to your Intention.

11

Frequency of Intention

After my husband and I had been together for about six months (the amount of time that covers a lot of people's initial infatuation), a classic dynamic began to play out. My husband, once he became comfortable and secure with me in his life, moved his attention to a day-to-day routine of watching TV, working, and training kids to box. I was putting out a lot of love, affection, and attention, and not receiving much back. Our idea of a big night out together became one of staying in and watching the Friday Night Fights.

This routine made me feel sad and isolated. At times, my husband would check out completely, and it was as if I didn't exist. I felt abandoned and in pain, but I knew that deep down the pain was actually his, because he had been abandoned by his biological father at a young age. His situation was not unlike what I lived through with my own father—also a man who had been abandoned in his youth and who had subjected me to that pain. In both cases, I felt unseen.

When I sought my husband's attention, sometimes even asking him if he still wanted to be with me, he blamed our issues on his perception that I was insecure. Furthermore, his fear of being overtaken by me led to even greater resistance on his part. He felt that whatever he did would make him wrong, and the situation fed on itself. We were in a constant state of entanglement and recrimination.

During this time, I was beginning to develop the tools of my practice and to discover the real nature of these kinds of seemingly unsolvable problems. On a day that I was especially depressed, I set my space on an episode from earlier in my life when I had fallen in love for a brief period of time and the world had seemed perfect. I imagined a Diamond out in front of me based on that feeling, and I started to put my Intention and my frequency and vibrations into this Diamond to create a new reality. The image of the Diamond was perfect because a Diamond reflects and refracts light, and it contains all the colors of the rainbow. I obtained a crystal, similar in properties to an actual Diamond, and I was looking at it and setting my Intention through it, when sunlight shone on the spot where I still keep it on my desk, illuminating it. I closed my eyes, and the Diamond light appeared to me in the center of my forehead. As it started to fade, I covered my eyes with my hands and the light came back, this time in shades of green and magenta. Then it shifted to blue, then purple, then pink. I opened my eyes again, and when I looked at the crystal on my desk, I could see the same colors reflected in real space. I began to set my Intention, continuing this exercise until my internal light became constant and I understood that my energy creates the reality around me.

My relationship with my husband changed into a new reality through my being able to see that when I had been moving my Attention outside myself to him, I had been agreeing to heal his pain. But by moving my Attention to the Diamond, I was moving into agreement with myself, thus creating a new reality, which was one of being present and passionate with joy and peace. Once I took my Attention off my husband and committed it to my true state of being, everything changed. I let go of the lie that my partnership was with him and became in agreement with the higher purpose of my life and my relationship with God. My family and our home life are now joyful, peaceful, and grounded.

To be successful at creating for ourselves, instead of trying to become successful, we need to be in the frequency of success. "Trying" to become successful is a process of matching the energy, the expectations, "the Pictures" if you will, of the people around you, and subsequently of the broader world on a horizontal plane. The "frequency" of success is a total state of being.

Setting ourselves in the internal frequency of our Intention is the basis for achieving whatever external changes we might seek. This process involves changing the energy inside ourselves so that it will emanate directly from its source in a positive way.

What happens when you *try* to be positive? The behavior is short-lived and winds up in resistance to being negative, and the harder you try to stop being negative, the stronger that behavior becomes in opposition. The energy and frequency you are sitting in ultimately drive the body's behaviors. If you try to change your behavior without changing your internal energy, you are setting yourself up for failure. That is why positive thinking, alone, doesn't work.

What happens when we *try* to be successful or achieve our Intention? Most people want to be successful. It's like wanting to be positive. When many of us declare our Intention to be positive, we mean that we're coming from a negative place to begin with and trying to do the opposite. But as long as we approach our Intention from a negative space, we will continue to create a reality wherein we lack the things we desire, no matter how hard we try to succeed.

What happens when we *try* to change? Do we take action to change our behaviors, or do we try to think differently? When we take action, often we're coming from a place of what we resist in ourselves. The moment we decide to be a certain way, we set ourselves up for the opposite to happen, because when we create with the energy of what we don't like about ourselves, we will go into resistance. Ironically, in other words, when we try to go to the positive side, our Backspace Pictures will affect us even more strongly.

Often, people find themselves trying to become a certain kind of person instead of simply being that person. Many people create drama in their lives and swing from negative behavior to what they consider positive because it makes them feel alive. By creating movement in this way, however, they wind up stuck in a battle between opposites.

Many books describe the habits of successful people. The problem with all of this is that if we don't match the frequency of success and try to change the source of our behavior, the body goes into resistance. What behaviors do we try to change—drinking, eating, procrastinating, addiction? Do our efforts succeed? By focusing on the external, we turn all of these efforts into a constant source of conflict and resistance. To be successful, we first must go to the frequency of what we want. Then our minds can observe and move us to what we don't want. The ultimate goal is wholeness, and we can achieve it by moving our attention to the Heart. Doing so will bring the opposites of what we want and don't want into relationship and make them whole. This is how we "be" a frequency, always in movement and never stuck. The choice is yours. It is your decision to say, "I unify the field of the positive and negative into the Greater Whole."

To be in a new internal frequency, we must clear our attachments to both the things that we want and that we don't want. In the process of doing this, we must look for the Pictures that are attached to the word *my* because we are defining ourselves by those Pictures: *my job, my body, my car, my relationship.* Then we must consider the abstract idea that in order for us to exist, someone has to be observing us. Our problem arises when they observe us through their own distortion, and we proceed to match that image. We ultimately can't rely on the people around us in that regard because if we align and connect with them on the basis of their distorted Pictures, we become stuck and live their reality. We are all experts in matching the energy that family and other people have brought into our space. The energy we need to match to move freely toward our true being and Intention is the energy that exists independently of the perception we have of ourselves through others. So, we must unify so that we and others can see ourselves in that new reality and space, instead of looking for others to see us this way.

We have to see ourselves Unified and Whole so that others can see us that way as well.

How do we get stuck in our lives? We get stuck when we are in a frequency that is matched to the external world, and no matter how hard we try to change, we remain stuck because we don't know how to see. When we see the light of Spirit within ourselves, then we can see that we are unified and whole. And when you allow that light to shine brightly, everyone then sees the Picture you are being.

We get stuck in a particular energy frequency because we have attached our identity to someone or something. Our parents, our ancestors, and our environment have programmed us, and the self-image that results is tuned into that frequency. Families and other groups get into agreement on Pictures of others. To change our energy frequency, we must change these Pictures. We change our energy and frequency based on wanting other people to see us, but they can't because we can't even see ourselves.

The only way for people to see us is to see our light within.

The Pictures in our space are so strong that they create the body's automatic responses. The body's responses, in turn, determine what we create.

Before we're born, we're at an energetic starting point that brings us into the world through the vibration of our genetic line. A new field of science called *epigenetics* is establishing the fact that our ancestors and their environmental influences vibrate within us. This is a part of the current that we move in.

In the womb, the only sound we're aware of is the beating of the Heart. Then we're born into a family, and the programming of who we are begins. We only know ourselves by what is reflected back to us and by the energy we experience around us. The frequency we vibrate in is that of our parents, our genetic line, and our culture. It's like a sea of cross currents that move through us. We feel the movement and we think it's us, but it's really a bombardment of frequencies that come at us. Our goal is not to collapse into these outside frequencies, but to set our own. Setting our frequencies will move us out into the world and onto the path of our higher self.

Families and cultures have certain Pictures, or self-images, that they operate by. This is the programming that naturally drives us. A problem occurs when we think we *are* those Pictures and we feel that energy, or we have judgment about the Pictures, which creates resistance, which activates the Pictures. We may think this is us because it's what we've been taught or conditioned to know. We think we know who we are based on the energy in our space, when in reality, what we really perceive is just a reflection of others around us. We may think we have free will, but the frequency we have been tuned into drives us to play out and create our own version of reality. We think we have a choice, but the energy driving us is stronger than our minds. If we identify ourselves as our Pictures, we don't change—we become stuck.

To be free, we must clear our Pictures by letting go of all attachments and judgments of who and what we think we are and what we aren't. The mind will try to drive our attention to define ourselves so that our egos can continue to exist as an extension of the things around us. But, to know who we really are, we must move inward, letting go of the process of identifying ourselves through the ego's attention to the external.

The mind wants us to identify who we are, so it can feel safe and know its place, but the moment we define our space is the moment we start to match a frequency, and if we define our space as the world around us, we will wind up in duality, trying to draw positivity from a negative space. We must clear the Pictures we are responding to in our space. We must let go of all our Pictures and move back to the zero point, the vibration without definition, which is found in the Heart.

Being in a positive frequency is not defining it, but "being" it. If we are something, we never have to try to create that thing. We are just being.

Can you ever try to define what the Unified Field is? The moment you attempt to define it is the moment it changes. It is everything you cannot begin to define. It is energy and vibration in motion, and it is because it is. Just like God says, "I am that I am."

Client Story

My client Bill runs a financial company and handles large sums of investors' money. One of Bill's key employees was anxiety-oriented and continually focused on why things might not work out. This employee spent a great deal of his time justifying his actions and was always in defense mode when Bill needed clarification or movement on an issue. When Bill set the Intention of the firm, the other employees were affected by this other person's negative attitude. He operated from fear.

I emphasized to Bill that for a new reality to be created, there must be an agreement. It is the agreement that will create the new reality. We had to have a focus, and that was the Intention that Bill had for his company. I told him that this Intention represented the Picture of what he wants and what vibration or frequency he wants the company to be in. Bill and I set the Intention as passion, confidence, and success. Bill set blue and red as colors for the frequency.

I told Bill to continue to be in present time with each day's new Intention. Also, once something in his world reflected what he *didn't* want, Bill needed to update that Picture to bring it into present time to what he wanted.

I told Bill, "If you are stressed, then it is a very bumpy ride. If you are in joy, it is like rolling through the hills. If you are vibrating in success, you are flying in a jet. It is important that you set the frequency so that everyone is moving and surfing the same wave you are. Everyone moves in different vibrations, but when you set a Picture and the vibration of that Picture, everyone then moves to the Picture and collapses into the reality you've set. You don't have to carry them or push them. It's effortless."

This Picture was the one that I told him his employees must play to. There could be no other Picture because it would compete, and he'd be living in someone else's reality. Bill committed with me to the idea that there is only one reality in his business and other people would have to match and be in it.

Bill needed to set and be in the vibration of confidence, passion, and success. I had him imagine a Diamond in the center of his office and had him put his Pictures of the goals he had for his business in the center of the Diamond. I had him set the Diamond at red and the field around the Diamond at blue. I then had him set the frequency of confidence, passion, and success, and we connected the Diamond to the Unified Field and the planet, letting wave energy move out through the office to invite the employees to join him. He asked them what their own goals were and whether they matched his. They had a choice of being in agreement with creating the new reality or to add to the new reality of a safe, secure, stable, and supported environment that could benefit everyone. He wanted them, more than anything, to understand that their goals and his were in alignment.

After the work we did, things changed dramatically. Bill and his problem employee uncovered a hidden dynamic that related to a father-son scenario of being seen and validated. But once we succeeded in getting everyone's focus on the true Intention of their work together and moving in the same vibration, personal dynamics ceased to be played out. The Diamond unified everyone into agreement.

ENERGYWORKS METHOD

1. ***Set and tune into the energy frequency of what you want.*** What is your Intention? You can say whatever you want to create in your life—for example, "I am rich . . . competent . . . a problem solver . . . in love . . . successful." Notice the vibration of your Intention. What color is it? Notice how you feel based on this Intention. Notice how your body responds. Does the Intention move your body to take action? Does it give you more energy? Does it quiet your mind? Move into the Picture of your Intention and observe your body from this frequency. Be this frequency NOW. Feel what it feels like. From this space of being, observe your body and let it vibrate like a gong to match that frequency. The observation creates the reality.

   Observe that you are already in this reality, and have your body match it.

Say to your body, "Match and multiply." See how long you can be here before the mind attaches to something else and pulls you out of the space. Watch what Picture your mind goes to, and then let go of that Picture by striking the gong, emptying the mind, and being in the vibration. Now move back into the Heart. Observe your Intention out in front of your space again. Notice if there is a difference between your body and your Intention.

2. ***Clear the energy frequency that you don't want.*** Are you in one place but would rather be somewhere else? Are you with one person but would rather be with someone else? Do you match the Picture of what you don't want? Are you anxious? Do you feel depressed? The reason is that your mind and energy are split. The first step in changing something is to be okay with what shows up, to observe it without attaching to it, and to accept the situation you're in in the moment without judging it. This way, you can have insight into what your energy has created. Your main goal here is not to split your mind and your energy so that you can let go of what you've created in the past. When you attach to a Picture, you match its energy and become that frequency. If you haven't let go of a Picture, notice that you're attached to it. Notice when you're in a situation and you'd rather be somewhere else. This feeling creates chaos because there's no alignment of the frequency and the Picture, and you're taken out of the moment and put in two places at once. To become unstuck, be in the frequency of being, and all your Pictures will disappear. This is how you

unify. You must become good at choosing new and different frequencies without attaching to the Pictures of that moment. Imagine sitting in your Heart. You are on a raft. Move through the circuit that connects your Heart to your Intention Space and back. Imagine you are lying in the sun as you float down this river into the golden light of your Intention. Feel how good it feels to be in this energy. As you leave the frequency of your Intention and move back into the Heart, you are coming back to the zero point. This is an empty slate. Notice how this space is different; notice how it is the void; notice how it is empty. This is the space of being that exists in the Heart. Now, allow your mind to move you out to the Intention of what you want and be in that frequency. Drop your mind back down into your Heart. Now, let the mind go and let it move to your Intention. What Intention are you attached to? To *be* in a frequency, you are not attaching to anything or anyone. Let it go and then you can experience it.

3. ***Be and move in the frequency of the Heart.*** Be in the Diamond of your Heart. It is from this place that you can be free of your Intention and not identify it as you. See the Picture of your Intention. The Heart is about freedom. The moment you define your space, you are no longer free. Remember, the moment you attach to something, you become trapped, you lose your freedom, and you define yourself by what you are attached to. Be right where you are in present time: focused and letting your Heart create the waves that move you in and out to your Pictures. Remember also that the Heart is what gets it done. The Heart is the fuel that moves us to the

horizon of the Intention. The Heart creates wave energy and, depending on how we are vibrating, the Heart is what gets us where we want to go. If your frequency is stress, you're moving on a very bumpy road. If your frequency is joy, it's like rolling through the hills. If your frequency is success, you are flying in a jet. It is important that you set the frequency so that everyone is moving and surfing the same wave you are to the reality you are creating. Everyone moves in different vibrations, but when you set a Picture and the vibration of that Picture, everyone then moves in and out to the Picture and collapses into the reality you've set. You don't have to carry them or push them. It's effortless.

4. ***Create from the whole by aligning the frequency of the Unified Field, through the Heart, to the frequency of the planet, to create your new reality.*** If you get out of agreement to being defined by other people and the limits of your mind, you can open up to new possibilities, and you will experience being and moving. When you align and get into agreement with what the Unified Field wants to create in you, you can allow your Intention to be released so that something new can come through. Agree to approach every situation in terms of being open and not knowing. When you don't have preconceived knowledge about something, you approach every situation as new. When your mind defines something, like your Intention, it limits who you are and what you can create because the mind is creating from the Backspace and Pictures of your past. So, open your mind to all possibilities and open your Heart to the frequency of the Field. When you open your Heart

to the Unified Field, you become a reflection of all things, and all things are possible. When you align and get into agreement with the planet, you can let go of whatever doesn't serve you. You'll be letting go of negative energetic patterns and behaviors. This grounds you and connects you so that you can manifest the agreement with the Unified Field that allows you to grow and create. You won't know who you really are until you interact with the Unified Field. When you become a reflection of the Unified Field, you are not defined by the past or by others. Your agreement with the Unified Field and the planet will create your new reality. You will be like a river—always flowing, being, moving, changing, growing, and transforming. You will respond to the world around you in a spontaneous way. You'll say and do things that you never knew you could. You will be in relationship with life and in the moment. You will dance through life as it changes every day. You will live your true Intention.

Journaling

Write down what you want. Draw a circle to the left of your list, and scratch and scribble all the energy that you don't want to contain it. The energy that you don't want has to move somewhere so the paper can contain it for you. Now, be in the frequency of your Heart and feel what it feels like to have what you want.

Body Movement

Grab an object or a stone that you can carry with you for the day. Set it with your Intention. Move the vibration and frequency of the Intention in the stone so that you can vibrate in that frequency throughout the day. The more you set objects at the frequency of what you want to be, the more external support you will receive because the external will now start to match the internal. Another exercise is to hold, in your right hand, the list of what you want (or just imagine it) and move your hand out and around and back to the Heart in a circle. Then either write down what you don't want and drop it to the ground from your left hand, or say out loud what you don't want and unify the two in an Infinity Loop. After this, say what it is you are now being—for example, "I am being love." "I am being joy." "I am being financially independent."

12

Playing the Game

During my childhood friendship with Louise, who could see light as I could, Louise started taking care of horses, and I would go along with her to help clean the stables. Then Louise met a woman who let us actually ride her horses and that was how we proceeded to spend all of our free time.

Being connected to horses was incredible. They were intuitive, like Louise and me. I could talk to the horse I was taking care of and feel that it understood me. The horses also seemed to sense the "space in between" because they, too, could read Pictures. They were Arabians, a spirited breed, and they would react to changes of energy, depending on who was around them.

I remember one woman who used to beat her horse as a way to try to control it. The horse hated her, and her energy was so bad that I would get a stomachache when I was around her. She was surrounded by black energy, and the horse would rear up every time she got on it. Finally, her horse threw her, and she injured her neck and couldn't ride. I was happy in a weird way because I'd felt so badly for the horse.

I started riding English style, and when the stable had horse shows, I would participate. I would communicate to Smoky, the horse I was taking care of, through mental Pictures. I would share with him Pictures of what we were going to do, and he would respond to them. I was learning how to jump at the time. I'd communicate a Picture of the obstacle we were going to jump over, and he would communicate back to me through movement.

This time in my life was great. Smokey often had a beautiful blue energy around his head that I could actually see, and I felt completely connected to him, even though I got to ride him only twice a week. The rest of the time, I would clean out the stalls and take care of the barn to pay my way.

I related to the way horses reacted to different environments. They sometimes got spooked or responded to people with bad energy by rearing or fidgeting. In turn, they responded calmly and affectionately when people would connect to their Hearts, communicate with them, and get into relationship with them.

The stables were about two miles from Louise's house, so in the summer we'd meet and walk there every day. I remember we had dreams of becoming jockeys even though, at eleven and fifteen, we were both already too big. Louise would read to me from books about legendary thoroughbreds like Man o' War, Seabiscuit, or Affirmed because I couldn't read them myself. She'd read to me every day, and we'd fantasize that someday we'd have our own horses. If we could have, we would have slept in the stables.

When I was with horses, I felt as if I were on a boat flowing over smooth waves. I seemed to lose track of time and felt alive and present. I was surrounded by positive energy. Eventually, I learned to put my energy to work for me and use it to elevate and transform my life.

Agreement creates reality, and everything is an extension of our own energy. What is our energy doing? How is it affecting the people around us? What reality is our energy creating? In the game of life, we have to know that wherever our energy goes is what we create, or, as explained above, "I create as I speak."

We all run our energy into the people, animals, and situations around us, and everything becomes an extension of our own energy in the process. Likewise, the energy that other people run toward us can take us over, and we, as a result, become an extension of them. But like my relationship with the horse, when we are connected via our hearts, communicating and in agreement, we co-create our own reality. Reality is based on an agreement. Just like a team agrees to play together to create a reality that elevates everyone to play with enthusiasm, courage, and a common goal, we achieve our own joy and Intention by moving and focusing from a place of agreement. We can agree only when we operate from our own true purpose. Otherwise, we are not in agreement; we are simply caving into someone else's reality.

Client Story

I have a client whose mother is a pathological narcissist. We've all known someone like this. Whatever the topic of conversation in a room or between two people might be, they instinctively and relentlessly figure out a way to make it about themselves. My client's mother was oblivious to the important events in her daughter's and granddaughter's lives but insisted on their complete attention to her own concerns. She'd create plans in which she demanded her daughter's participation, and then, with no forethought whatsoever, would cancel them after the work and commitment that the plans required were well underway. As a result of this constant diversion of energy, my client would lose her focus on life whenever she conversed with her mother. In fact, she had so much anxiety built up in anticipation of dealing with her mother's perpetual self-absorption and demanding attitude that she'd have physical symptoms of indigestion every time she picked up the phone and heard her mother's voice.

My client was left in a state of chaos and confusion after each such conversation, and this state carried over into all of her relationships. She lacked support on every level: from her mother, to her business associates, to the husband she eventually divorced.

Over the years my client reacted to this situation by setting up a controlling environment for herself and the people around her to achieve stability. She became a professional accountant by trade, specifically because it was a way to work in a system where the very product consisted of flawless mathematical balance. Her private life was similarly controlled, and her family was subjected to a life of military-level regimentation. Through all of this, her internal system remained in the same state of perpetual chaos and uncertainty. It was like a wave that started with her mother and spread out.

I knew that in order for her to change, my client had to go back to the source of this chaos, which was the treatment she got from her parents. I told her that to approach her mother in a positive way she needed to set up a game, with the object being to grow and prosper as her ultimate goal, and then for her to follow the steps for mastering it.

My client had to create her own playing field, put on her game face, keep her eye on the ball, and master the game. In doing these things, my client was able to regain her focus and move her life forward. She learned to clarify her own Intention and not simply respond to her mother's.

Her Intention had to be self-supportive. On a team, the only way that teammates can rely on each other is for every teammate to demonstrate the skills, confidence, and willingness to handle their part of the action.

My client had to establish her game face. She had to set the wave energy from her Heart and ride that wave onto the playing field. She had to be perceived as both a source and a receiver of support.

She also had to keep focused on the ball, which is another way of saying that she had to know her true Intention. On a team, each player has to be aware of their own position and the other players' positions on the field, and at all times they must remain focused on the ball. Furthermore, there must be an unqualified willingness and commitment to sharing the ball—passing it back and forth in a way that moves the whole game forward. My client's mother hogged the ball, and in doing so she blocked the progress of the game to suit her own selfish and counterproductive ends. No one can win in any true sense of the word when this happens, and on a good team, that kind of player is rejected.

It's a cliché, but my client had to understand that the game isn't exclusively about winning or losing: It's about how you choose to play, and getting lost in doing so; it's the space of getting lost where you truly create. Having said that, mastering the game and playing it well make the satisfaction of winning automatic. The result of winning, in my client's case, allowed her to regain her focus and move her life forward. She rode a wave of support, created by relationships with people who are, by their very nature, supportive, because she learned to support herself.

Immersion in this kind of thinking and feeling has vastly improved my client's life. The support that she now generates from her inner self-confidence and emotional stability is consistently reflected back from her friends, family, and colleagues. Her income has tripled, she's moved with her daughters from a shabby apartment to a beautiful house, and most importantly, she no longer gives her energy away to her mother. And, believe it or not, her mother has done a total about-face and now extends herself and shows up and gives to my client and her children, being there in a whole new way.

Energy is the source of power that we use to accomplish our goals or create our Intention. How are you using your energy? Do you use your energy to do what you want, or do you give it to others? How much of your energy can you access to accomplish your Intention? Remember, if you are participating in a situation or scenario, you're in agreement with creating that reality, and your energy is the thing that is holding it together.

Your energy is the most valuable resource you have, and by mastering the right tools, you can use, direct, move, and change it. Here are four game-analogous steps that constitute a simple approach to claiming and controlling your energy. Remember that winning doesn't mean beating the other guy. It means freeing yourself to learn, to grow, to move forward, and to own your own space.

ENERGYWORKS METHOD

1. ***Choose your own playing field.*** Imagine a Diamond out in front of you. Imagine the energy from the Unified Field coming down into the Diamond. This is the source of energy that allows you to play your game. Now imagine energy coming up from the planet and moving into the Diamond like an erupting volcano. The Heart creates in a circle in a field around you that looks like a bubble. This is the field you play on; it's the horizontal and vertical. Let this physical energy combine with the Spiritual energy from the Unified Field. Move the energy out from the Diamond onto your playing field. Focus on your breath as you start to inhale. Now, choose a color for your playing field that sets the agreement of how you want to play. On my playing field, I set the colors blue and gold. I want to be on a playing field with people who play in peace and harmony. Breathe in the blue energy of clarity. As you exhale, breathe out the gold energy of inspiration. Unify the two of those and allow your mind to go blank. Breathe and drop into the Heart with no thought.

2. ***Put on your game face.*** When you find yourself in a situation that you want to change, focus on the tip of your nose to pull your attention inward so that your energy returns to you and your power resides in your personal space. When you're confronted with someone from your past, they won't know you in this new reality and they'll begin to play out the old one, but it's up to you to stay focused so that you can change. Remember that agreement creates

reality. You are inviting them onto a new playing field. They may not be able to play on this field with you, but you'll know within five minutes. If they can't play on the field of clarity and inspiration, end the conversation and try again tomorrow. It's easy to give up your energy to other people because you may want to heal them or help them, but what you are doing is giving your energy away. The playing field creates an opportunity to play a new game with the people we already know, but it also opens us up to meeting new people who can play in this new space. Remember, this playing field is not about the other person; it is about your Intention and remaining focused on the ball.

3. ***Keep your eye on the ball***. On this playing field, you're going to focus on the Intention of what you want. This is the ball. Be aware of your breath as you start to breathe in the blue energy of clarity and exhale the golden energy of inspiration. The trick here is not to make the game about yourself or the other person. It's about focusing, playing, and moving to the ball, which is how you create happiness, peace, and joy. When we focus on the ball, we lose the mind, we play the game, and we create something new. This movement is where we experience happiness and create a new reality. When we make the game about the ball, which is our Intention, we forget about ourselves, we forget about the other person, and a third energy comes into play: the energy of the Heart. This is where we experience the Greater Whole.

4. ***Master the game***. By creating your own playing field, you will channel positive energy and be able to change the way you interact with others. When you play in and out of what you want and don't want, you won't get attached to either one, and you'll keep moving through the field of play. We need to communicate and be in relationship with our body. If the game of life starts pummeling you and you need a break, ask the soul to slow down so the body can catch up. The soul can create what you want in an instant, but the body needs to play through this field of opposing energy at its own rate. Agreement creates reality. To play the game of life, we have to focus on the ball, which is our Intention. The moment we agree to create a reality, the Spirit matches that frequency. The trick is to bring this frequency into the body so that we can manifest our dreams. To do that, we must have communication between the body and the being. The Heart is what makes this possible. True creation happens when we can just be in communication with where we are in the game. Whether it's in the sand trap or on the green, we are still moving with and focused on the ball. Playing the game is what enables us to create, and the more we do it, the better we get.

Journaling

Draw a Diamond and write your Intention in it. Draw a sun and draw a connection cord from the Diamond up to the sun. Draw a planet and draw a connection cord down to the planet. Draw a figure eight. Unify the vertical playing field. Now, draw a horizontal Infinity Loop between your Intention Space (what you do want) and the Backspace (what you don't want). As you are moving your pen through what you want and don't want, pause in the Diamond space and just be there for a while; then keep moving your pen through the vertical and horizontal loops as a way of moving through the field. That is how you get in the game.

Body Movement

Keep your eye on the ball, which is your Intention. Like playing a game of golf, even if you are in the sand trap, keep playing to your Picture. If you are in a Picture you don't like, draw a Picture of it, or write down a description, crumple up the piece of paper, and throw it away.

13

Spontaneous Creation

When I was a very little girl, I could see waves of light energy moving through the space between objects. It took the form of sparkling bubbles that would float and then connect to other bubbles, creating communication and constant interaction in a relationship that would culminate in a huge wave. I always had a sense of peace and connection when I'd look at the light energy. I'd perceive it as something alive—constantly moving, changing, evolving, and growing.

At night, I'd look at the stars and connect each star like dot-to-dot. The stars would seem to create patterns and shapes, unique to me at that age, because I knew nothing of constellations. Sometimes I would see monster shapes, and other times I'd see animals or people. Then, suddenly, I would see shooting stars, and sometimes it seemed as though I was at a fireworks show, watching the lights exploding above me.

I would see one star pulsating and then another star pulsating, and it seemed as though the stars were communicating with each other, creating a network or web that connected them all. At this point, I started to place my Intentions, or my goals, into Diamonds. To the Diamonds above, those stars in the sky, I would make a wish for something that I wanted. There was an endless supply of stars and an endless supply of wishes.

Diamonds speak louder than words. They are like stars that reflect and refract light, which is a form of communication. When I'd see a shooting star, I'd make a wish and would try to follow the light and imagine where it would land on the planet. If a shooting star moved, I knew the corresponding wish would come true. In this way, I felt that the light of the stars was communicating with me down on the planet.

The stars, the Diamonds in the sky above, reflect connectivity and the network of the whole. The plants and trees in the ground reflect the network of roots through which the natural world connects and communicates. Connecting the "above" with the "below" are feedback loops that pass through the Heart that we must engage with in this world to be able to create. We've always possessed the clues and signs for accomplishing this, but since we live in the mind and not in the Heart, we've forgotten how.

As a grownup, I've come to understand that this is how I suddenly "popped," or had a spontaneous experience of the way things evolve and are created. To create, there must be a space to create in, like the universe or sky above. From this space, Pictures spontaneously emerge. They are like the bubbles, or the Diamonds in the sky, or the seeds in the ground. When we create a connection to these different spaces, communication begins, and from this communication we create a circuit and network that continue to evolve based on the whole. When we create from the Heart, we create from the Whole, and creation from the Whole is spontaneous. Instantaneous shifts in reality can happen.

When we create from the mind, we're limited to a linear process and set of directions. However, when we create from the Heart, we can make an evolutionary jump, and through the process of "popping," we can create connections to a new reality. These connections can be activated and create a network that explodes outward from the Heart in every direction. When we create from the Wisdom of our Hearts, we embark on a new playing field, and the game we pursue is a love affair with life.

In the process I call "popping," the spontaneous shift happens. Through it, we can open up to the Wisdom of the Heart to reveal a new reality and create from the Greater Whole.

As a little girl, I was often criticized for getting too excited and was told to calm down. I would jump around with enthusiasm about creative ideas that were occurring in me, but these ideas would then be unrelated to the next idea that came along. This behavior would frustrate my teachers and the other people around me, and they would tell me to focus on something, often snapping at me and deflating my enthusiasm. I felt misunderstood, so I shut down and had a hard time expressing myself. I could never follow my thoughts in a sequential or linear manner, no matter how hard I tried. I felt like a failure.

I was given medication like Adderall to enhance my ability to focus, and it did help me focus, but it also left me feeling ungrounded and "speeded up," so I got off it soon thereafter. Living in a linear world is extremely complicated for the numerous people who have ADD or

ADHD. These people are trying to conform to the life of the mind. They have never been shown how to use their gift for spontaneous creation because in the linear world they have to survive, and their nonlinear connection is considered a handicap.

One day, much later in my life, I was in my garden talking to a friend about insights that I had been experiencing. My thoughts were all over the place, popping like popcorn, rapidly and randomly. In the middle of the conversation, my friend said, "Can you just focus?"

I noticed that, in that moment, my enthusiasm dropped, and I felt as if I was being controlled, constricted, and limited. I felt my creativity leave. My friend wanted me to look at one Picture because she could see me only from that Picture. In this way she could use her Picture of me as a way of feeling in control. She couldn't see me from the Whole, but could see me only as the friend who would heal and give to others.

I could suddenly see that through communicating and talking about all of my different ideas and the various things that came up through this process of spontaneously creating, connections and networks for them came to life. Something new and unknown was coming in. It was an "aha" moment, and my friend had cut off the creative flow. When we create, the people around us can go into fear. If I start to pop in my family space, my husband and two boys will start to criticize me and put me down because I have moved out of their Pictures of wife and mother, thereby ungrounding their reality.

Earlier, my friend had told me about her frustration with her partner. He felt that she was always trying to control him or pull him down while he was creating. I told my friend to let her partner pop. It's his form of creation. It's how he's able to raise his vibration to the stars and then come back into the Heart to create new realities. This creativity is reflected in art, in music, and in the environment. High levels of creativity don't happen because people are thinking about wanting to create something. They happen when people sit in the stillness of the Heart and something new emerges.

I told my friend that the next time her partner "popped," to let him pop, and then try to see what new insights or energy came through. It's a creative process, and when creation comes in this way, it's like a rapid burst of energy that spews and fills up the space like fresh popcorn, transcending verbal communication. It becomes the process of creating in Pictures. The Pictures create a field of energy, and if that energy, channeled from a higher place, is brought back down to the Heart, suddenly there's no thought at all—just creation. We are connecting, dot-to-dot, from our Heart, forming these Pictures to create a network that activates a new reality.

By learning the tools of spontaneous "popping" from the Heart, we can create new Pictures, connect to them, move to them, and activate them. It is through this communication that the circuit builds a relationship of where we are to where we want to go.

When we live in the Heart, we create from the Whole and experience the world from wholeness. By occupying the Heart, we bring in the unknown, and a new reality can be created instantaneously around us. We must know how to move and create in our garden, and the more connections and communicating relationships we make with these new realities, the more our network will expand and reflect on the people we encounter so that they can experience the same spontaneous shift. It is through this constant connection, communication, and co-creation that something greater gets created.

The process of popping is a way to spontaneously create. Many of us don't have the space available to create in because the people we are around try to control or direct us. They see us in a linear way by defining us as a Picture of what they want us to be so that they can feel safe. When we change who we are, we may make many people around us angry because we are getting out of agreement with a reality they want to create.

When we move our energy up into the sky and then move it back to our Hearts, we create a circuit that is moving and connecting us to a new reality. By learning the tools of spontaneous popping from the Heart, we can create Pictures, connect to them, and activate them through communication, creating a network that will connect us all.

To take a spontaneous jump, we must move our Intentions way out into the stars to observe a new field of energy. This gives us the perspective to see the whole Picture and not just the pieces. We can see how random thoughts and ideas may connect together and how things are connected in the network of light.

To know how to read a field of energy, we have to connect the dots of seemingly unrelated Pictures. Events are a form of communication, giving us clues as to what we are consciously and unconsciously creating. By identifying what Pictures come up, we are communicating with our internal world, gaining insight that enables us to learn and grow, so that we can let go of what we don't want and spontaneously create something new.

Client Story

I had a client who couldn't let go of a recently ended relationship. We always focused on his career in our sessions, and he didn't want to create relationship Pictures. One day, I asked him to simply identify all of the Pictures connected to this relationship, and I got him to talk about each Picture. He said, "We had fun together and great sex. We fought hard, but we played hard. She was insecure, and my family didn't like her because of her emotional drama. She wanted kids, but I had kids already and didn't want more."

I told him to contain the space and consider the thoughts and emotions that were connected to these Pictures, then to put a bubble around passion, desire, laughter, fun, drama, anger, and jealousy. He moved the energy of what he wanted into a bubble. Like a rocket, he shot the bubble up into space to a star.

My client created space between himself and these Pictures so that he could observe them from a different viewpoint. He and his former partner had been in a power struggle to get what they wanted. They were trying to force a relationship but were two people with different goals. As such, they were trying to manipulate each other instead of being direct with their Intentions and recognizing their true Hearts' desires. When they were together, they were always divided, moving in and out of relationship. When we're divided, it means we don't have matching Pictures. In their case, they were kicking different balls in the game.

The couple broke up, but he kept drifting back to her and kept comparing other women he was dating to her. He continued to create a state of not being in relationship and of not finding anyone like her because he thought he couldn't have what he wanted. He was always focused on what he didn't want, and he continued to seek out encounters reflecting that.

I asked him, "In business, do you know what you want?"

He answered, "Absolutely."

"Do you go back and forth on deals?"

"Never."

"Do you want the deal and then don't want the deal? Are you indecisive?"

"No."

"Do you get sidetracked and lose focus on the deal?"

"No."

"Can you observe how your goal and the playing field in business are clear? How there is no drama, how it is fun, and how you love to play to your Pictures? Drama comes from confusion. It occurs when people are forcing a relationship around Pictures that don't match."

Through this conversation, my client finally gained insight that he and his partner had been on two different playing fields and that they were focused on different goals, neither being right or wrong.

I then asked, "What is your Intention for your relationship?"

He answered, "I have never owned my Intention. I want someone who already has kids or has no desire for kids. I want someone who wants to be free, someone who has fun, loves to play, is sexual, and who has her own life and interests, and who is Heart-connected and passionate about what she does."

I advised him to focus on the star, the new goal that went beyond his Intention to new possibilities—to let all the old Pictures fall to the planet, and to receive and own these new possibilities. I had him move the Diamond of his Heart up and connect it to the star. I got him to make a wish and to let that wish be like a shooting star that moved into his Heart and filled him up. And finally, I asked him to let this light spontaneously shift him and shift his energy to allow him to create something new. Within a month, he was in an ideal relationship.

ENERGYWORKS METHOD

1. ***Create a container or space.*** The first step in spontaneous creation is simply to sit in the space of the Heart, connected to Spirit above and grounded to the planet below. To spontaneously shift into a new reality, you must be in your Heart and run your energy vertically. The Heart is the bridge between Spirit above and planet below; and the Heart, like the network of roots in the earth, moves out in the horizontal world that connects, communicates, and co-creates with our Pictures that we don't get stuck in but change when we need to. The reason is that the Heart unifies the future and past (the field of time) and the negative and positive (the field of space). We are weaving our reality. The Heart brings the body and our being into union, and that is where the spontaneous shift of co-creation occurs. To create, there must be a space to create in, just like the blank canvas on which an artist paints. Be in the Heart. Imagine it as a Diamond within. Now, imagine the space in the sky as an empty space to create in. From this space Pictures spontaneously emerge. Light moves through this space in the blink of an eye and activates a network of energy. It is like you are projecting a light show from your Heart into the sky.

2. ***Create a connection and feedback loop.*** Identify the events and Pictures that have occurred in your day of what you want and don't want, and write them down. Contain these events, thoughts, and Pictures in a bubble by drawing them on a piece of paper or imagining them. Don't get into a conversation with them—just identify them.

   What you want: Focus on your Heart's energy as you move the bubble of your goal up to a star in the sky and let your wish go to the Unified Field so that you can co-create with it. Each time something that you want comes up that isn't in your current reality, contain it in a bubble and let go of it and direct it to a star. This is also a good exercise to do if you blow bubbles. See how the Unified Field will communicate and give feedback to what you are requesting by handing your wish over.

   What you don't want: Focus on your Heart's energy of what you don't want and contain it in a bubble. Move this bubble down into the Earth so you can let it go, and let the Earth recycle it and transform it into the physical manifestation of your wish. When we have a wish, in order for it to come true, we must also be in communication with the planet and let go of something that we are holding onto that may not serve us. Draw a bubble around what you don't want, contain the energy of it, and let it go so that something new can show up in a new form. After you complete this step, draw or write out the updated Picture of what you want and plant it in the ground like a seed.

3. ***Connect the dots.*** We've identified the Pictures, contained the energy, and created space. Now, connect the dots to see what your Pictures are telling you and how they are directing you to new insights. Draw or imagine a Diamond. Imagine all the Pictures and thoughts that have come up for you through this creative process as dots that can now be connected. Draw or imagine a connection from dot-to-dot and then focus on your Heart. Draw or imagine a line from the Diamond of your Heart to each dot, and then draw or imagine another line back from the Picture to the Diamond to represent a circuit. When everything is connected, you will have created a network of communication and light for activating a new reality. When we create a connection from the Diamond in the Heart to the Diamond in the sky, communication begins at a higher frequency, and from this communication a circuit and a network continue to evolve. Communication through light, which takes the form of Pictures, is instant, and instantaneous shifts in reality can occur. This is our feedback loop. Light reflects out and is reflected back, and in that connection something altogether new is activated. Moving energy in this circuit raises a vibration and then lowers the vibration back to the Heart. Each time you pop up, you hit another layer of energy and information, which provides insights to new realities. You become senior to all energy in your space. You have to get out of all of your old Pictures and become a King or Queen over your new reality so that your old Pictures no longer have an effect on you. As you move through this space, you'll change and grow. Creating isn't

about working through something with effort. It's about creating in the moment, and to create something new, you must go up into the Unified Field and bring that energy down into the body and Release something so that something new can grow. Connecting the dots that form the Pictures of a new reality is a creative process that facilitates this step. For example, once you set your new reality, say, "I have this new reality," and then start to create space to make a plan. Don't wait for it to happen.

4. ***Zoom in and zoom out.*** Like an artist working on a canvas, you need to step back on a regular basis to get an overview of the whole, all the while remaining focused on the details. We are focused on our Intention, but we constantly zoom out to view the broader landscape and the whole field of energy. Imagine looking through a pair of binoculars and adjusting the zoom. Pick an Intention to focus on and zoom in to see it in minute detail. Then zoom back out to view it in the broadest possible space. See how far away it is and then see how close. Zoom in so that the particular Picture is all that you see. Notice how you can't see anything else? Now zoom out and look at all the Pictures, like Diamonds or stars in the sky.

Throughout history, there have been moments of spontaneous creation. During the European Renaissance there was an explosion of art, music, and creativity that moved the soul, and the works of art that were created in that time and place reflected a new reality that put light back into the world. In the same way, we can bring light in through ourselves that will channel back to everyone around us.

Imagine all of the Pictures and Diamonds in the sky and what they're reflecting to you as if you have it all in the moment. What are they communicating to you? If you're focused on someone else, ask yourself, "What in them is being reflected to me about my creation?"

Our focus is always the whole picture. When we look at our Pictures, we need to see what the Pictures are telling us about which steps to take next. When we create space, we can see the whole, and the random Pictures that we encounter along the way give us insight into what our next steps should be, as long as we continue to learn. When we change the way we see something, the external Pictures change with it, and we spontaneously shift into a new and fulfilling reality.

Most ideas don't stick, or Intentions don't work, because there's not enough energy to connect them. The Heart creates a relationship, and in order for an idea to happen or a movement to occur, the Pictures that represent these things must take root in the Heart, where energy grows. Most Pictures don't happen because when a past Picture shows up, most people see it as reality, as opposed to something that is coming up and out of them. They believe the lie of their past that is in their space.

Journaling

Draw a circle that represents the Heart. Draw a line from that circle to another circle of what you want (writing down inside that circle what you want, even one word representing what you want). Then move back to the Heart circle and pop up and write down a line and circle of what you don't want. Your image will look like an octopus. Then alternate between what you want and don't want. Then draw a line to connect the dots and notice if any Pictures start to form. As you draw from what you want to the Heart to what you don't want, you really want to end up having no particular Pictures in the Heart so that you can be present in the moment for something new to come through.

Body Movement

Take two sheets of paper. On one sheet, write down what you want and throw it up in the vertical. Keep throwing it up. On the other sheet, write down what you don't want and throw it down to the planet. The right hand represents what you want, and the left hand represents what you don't want. Notice what comes up for you as you do this body movement.

14

Own Your Energy Balls, Own Your Power

Jesus said to them, "When you make the two into one, and when you make the inner like the outer and the outer like the inner, and the upper like the lower, and when you make male and female into a single one, so that the male will not be male nor the female be female, then you will enter in [the kingdom]."
(Gospel of Thomas: 22)

I have always tended to play on the feminine, passive side of the game, which is to say that people would boss me around, and I would become overtaken and do as they said. When my husband and I moved in with my in-laws at a time when we were remodeling our house, I finally "owned my energy balls."

What does "owning our energy balls" mean? It means owning the ground we stand on. It means bringing our masculine and feminine into balance and owning our space. Owning our crown allows us to spiritually know who we are and what we want. Owning our energy balls is owning our masculine and feminine energy so that we can become balanced and move physically on a playing field where our goals can be achieved.

We were only going to stay with my in-laws for a few months, but, as these things sometimes go, we ended up living with them for over a year. At the same time, Tony's older and younger brothers both moved back home, so seven of us were living in a three-bedroom house.

My husband comes from a large family, and the siblings are all boys. His mother, a college professor, is the matriarch, one of a long line of educators. I remember meeting them for the first time and thinking that they were all really short. My mother is 5'11", my father is 6'2", my brother is 6'5", and I have a 6'9" nephew, so I wasn't used to looking down on family members. My first impression was, "They're really nice, but they're short and bossy." They seemed to know everything and would speak with absolute certainty. They would also criticize other people's assertions and point out errors in logic as a way of establishing the fact that they were always right.

My husband's family would only understand things that were presented in a logical and sequential manner. This was challenging for me because they discounted everything I said. Their nickname for me was Hocus Pocus. Early on, I had a hard time with this opinion because my work was my expression of myself, and it was being disregarded and ridiculed. I'd become defensive, and they'd approach the resulting conversation with logic and rationalization.

I was surrounded by males and a mother-in-law who only ran masculine energy. She was uncomfortable with emotions and female creativity. In their family, females were dismissed as being emotional, dramatic, and chaotic, and would be labeled as "stirring the pot." These were the stereotypes I had to fight against. I don't think that my husband's family was aware of not acknowledging females, but when women spoke, no one listened. I found myself being talked over and not heard.

This was the year in which my playing field changed. I learned to "own my energy balls" and activate my masculine side to support my feminine so that she wasn't invalidated or treated like a second-rate citizen. Being in this family helped me own who I am and brought me into balance. I was being put down both subtly and directly, and I had to learn not to care what others thought. I had to learn not to be a victim and learn to own my power.

My husband's mother wouldn't waive her opinions, even under attack. She was out of balance because she didn't support either her feminine or the feminine side of people around her, male or female, unless they acted through the masculine. I am grateful for being in this family because it forced me to own my own masculine side and not be devastated by their comments. It taught me how to own my "energy balls." Later on, it didn't matter to me what they said about me and my work. In fact, they've all had sessions with me by now, and I've helped bring balance to the family. I put them directly in touch with their feelings and emotions to access and support the feminine within them.

When clients don't embrace their emotions and deny their feelings, when they don't know how to communicate, and when their responses are typically to ignore problems, I'm now able to be direct and to use my masculine side to bring their feminine out of hiding so that they can illuminate situations they would previously repress. I'm grateful to my husband's family for their presence with me on this playing field, where we bring our feminine and masculine into relationship. When these sides are in balance, it creates movement, and that is what we need to be able to change our lives.

I've been in this family for twenty years, and I was the first to find out that my husband's stepfather, the father who raised him, has a daughter that no one knew about. We are all afraid to bring the feminine out of hiding, and his stepdad was concerned about the possibility of losing his family. I have to applaud my mother-in-law's response to finding out about this and embracing her husband's daughter, in spite of being upset about his keeping her a secret. We hide things because they are a part of ourselves that we can't face. When this news came out, we made my husband's new stepsister our first son's godmother. She is now integrated into the family, but it took time for her father to own his feminine and celebrate her. This is just one interesting example of how we hide the female.

Here's another. Some years ago, my husband's youngest brother came out of the closet. He said to his parents, "I have two things I want to tell you. The first is that I've been practicing kickboxing for four years, and the second is that I'm gay." His father's response was, "Tell me about the kickboxing," at which his mom laughed out loud. The next morning, my mother-in-law came over to our house and told my husband that his brother was a gay kickboxer. My husband was shocked but was fully supportive. Apparently, his brother had been in a relationship with a partner for four years.

That morning, my brother-in-law sent us all emails, directing us to Facebook as a way of informing the rest of the family and the public at large. He came out about being gay with a picture of him and his partner. The family didn't understand why he hadn't told them and why they had to learn about it with the rest of the world. When asked, he referred to his dad, and replied, "I learned from the best."

The fact is that this family had a history of denying feelings and emotions. It was one more example of hiding the female side and keeping her locked up, unsupported, and without a voice. The following day, my father-in-law and my husband sent my husband's brother an email acknowledging his courage.

Finally, on our most recent group vacation, I was hugging my son because I'm very affectionate. My father-in-law said, "Stop that. It's making me uncomfortable." He had never hugged his kids or told them he loved them.

I said, "Okay, you're going to have hugging lessons. I know you can't do this with people, but we can start with a pillow pet." I gave him my son's pillow pet and said, "Hug it."

He was even uncomfortable giving the pillow a hug. I said, "For ten minutes you need to give that pillow a hug and some love." After he was done, I said, "Can you hug me?" He couldn't. I then said to my husband's mom, "It's your turn to learn to hug," and I gave her the pillow pet, too.

The next morning, I said to my father-in-law, "I'm going to give you a hug, and you don't have to give me a hug back. Just receive the hug." By the end of the week, he was hugging me, and the family was cheering him on. Now, he can't get enough, and I'm also hugging my mother-in-law these days.

Even in a family dynamic, balance is impossible if energy gets stuck in either the masculine or feminine, and a tendency to compensate for one or the other will create conflict. Because I have achieved balance by embracing my energy balls and owning my masculine side, I'm able to support and enhance my feminine side, allowing her to come out and fully integrate. This is also happening in my husband's family, where the feminine side is now being embraced, bringing the passive into the light.

Last Christmas, I gave my mother-in-law a pair of the energy balls I sell, as a way of helping her embrace the feminine within, and she loves them. As much as we were opposite when we first came together, we are now in agreement not to play one side against the other as we integrate ourselves into the Whole.

Owning our energy balls is about bringing into balance our masculine and feminine energy—the positive and negative, and the passive and active within all of us, so that we can own our power and move in the world. This is about activating our circuits so that our energy moves us. This is where there is unity, and this is where, by playing together, we can create from the Greater Whole.

Owning our energy balls is not about gender. It is not about being female or male. We all have within us masculine and feminine sides, but for centuries we have been playing the same boring game of duality, being separate and divided, stuck on one side or the other. To create something new, we need to be on a new playing field—one that will bring the masculine and feminine or the positive and negative sides within us into balance.

For females, by energy balls, we refer to the ovaries, the source of female creativity. Even if a woman has had a hysterectomy, the energy field of female creativity still resides in that space. Just by acknowledging this, female creativity is activated. For men, we're referring to the actual testicles and prostate. In both cases, the energy originates at the base of the spine and unifies in the crown above the head. We can activate and awaken the masculine and feminine energy at the base of the spine to achieve movement and own our power, creating a solid Foundation. If energy is moving, our life activates, and everything grows.

Females who don't own their energy balls, or masculine side, don't step onto the playing field or play to their goal. They sit on the sidelines, watching the masculine play from a distance. However, if we support our female side by owning our energy balls, our masculine side will bring us into harmony and balance, creating movement to take action toward our goals.

When we "own our energy balls," we are grounded to the planet. We nurture it, and it nurtures us as well. But when we reject our own feminine side, we reject Mother Earth, and this is when we get stuck. Being stuck on the feminine side means being scattered and not knowing what we want. Either we don't own our masculine side, or we are stuck in the masculine and are out of balance. We then fail to support the feminine.

Some of us must own our energy balls to be able to support the feminine within, thus bringing us into balance and harmony. Others must acknowledge their feminine energy to avoid being controlling and domineering, hurting themselves in the process, and the world as well.

Women, who bring forth life, have the power to create a new playing field, but females are often afraid of owning their masculine side because of centuries of conditioning. Culturally, they've been taught to believe that men won't be attracted to them if they exert their creative power. Powerful women are often viewed as controlling, domineering, cunning, and aggressive. There's a negative connotation placed on powerful females in the perception that they're too male. And it's true that women with dominant male characteristics often don't support their own feminine side or the feminine side of other women. They keep the female hidden like a Genie trapped in a bottle.

We've been playing a male-dominated game for centuries. It's a game of superior and inferior, of dominance and control, of the haves and have-nots. But all of us, whether we're male or female, need to support the feminine. By supporting the feminine, we acknowledge that she is the creator of life. Although she may not be seen as active or taking action, it's her creative energy that brings things into being. Yet we keep her hidden. We don't want to acknowledge this side of ourselves because it doesn't get validated in terms of immediate results, and it's harder to define what the feminine is accomplishing because it isn't always focused on the short term.

The key to unifying the two sides is to open to the Wisdom of the Heart. This is where the power lies. By opening to the Wisdom of the Heart, we unify the masculine and feminine. This is how our circuit gets activated at the base of the spine and moves up the vertical field to the crown. When we move our internal energy on the vertical plane, things instantly happen that can be seen manifested in the external world.

If we continue to play the old boring game of opposites on the horizontal field, we'll remain stuck. Playing this game consists of unconsciously trying to bring things into balance by looking for our opposite to move us, and this is what often attracts us to certain people, regardless of their gender. When we play this game in relationships, one person becomes the active, dominant side, and the other person, the passive. We may play out one side or the other but never fully activate and move to our purpose. If we're operating only in the masculine, we become dominant or controlling, and when we access only the feminine, we're unfocused, passive, and chaotic. Either way, we can't fully activate, and we lose our power.

We need to take back our power by owning our energy balls so that we can keep our bodies grounded to the planet and move with our own energy. To open up to the Wisdom of our Heart is to unify the masculine and feminine sides from above and below. Thus, when we play in the vertical, our world changes spontaneously in the horizontal.

Are you vulnerable, insecure, or doubting? Do you fail to seize opportunities? Do others take credit for your creative ideas? Are you indecisive? Do you suppress your emotions? If any of this is true, you need a set of energy balls.

On the opposite side of things, are you overly aggressive, domineering, controlling, or overbearing? If you have to be in control, the reason is that you haven't embraced your feminine side and you're not balanced. This means you'll prey on the vulnerable feminine, when what you're really seeking is balance for the masculine inside yourself so that you can move and create from the Whole.

It's a given that gender issues still exist in society. Femininity is by nature passive and receptive. Women receive sperm to create a baby. Their balls are their ovaries, and they're internal, whereas men's balls are external. Men, by nature, go outside for what they want. But the playing field won't change until both males and females activate movement by owning both their masculine and feminine sides.

Our energy is like a flashlight that has to have a battery with a negative and positive charge in order for the light to turn on. We have to know how to connect the battery into the negative and positive, the masculine and feminine, to create a charge so the energy completes a circuit.

Four poles need to be connected within our space to activate a charge so that we know how to move the energy in our body. One is located on the vertical plane, and two are located on the horizontal plane. The pole on the vertical runs from the top of the crown (the positive charge) to the base of the spine (the negative charge). The positive charge is powered by the connection with the Unified Field. The negative charge is grounded to the planet and keeps us safe and secure.

When we open to the Wisdom of the Heart, we activate and unify the masculine and feminine poles on the horizontal plane.

The other horizontal pole is the future-past pole that goes in front of the Heart and through the Heart to the Backspace. When we open to the Wisdom of the Heart, we activate and unify the future and past. This represents the Intention Space and Backspace. The Intention Space is the positive charge, and the Backspace is the negative charge. This is considered to be the Time Loop. The Space Loop, on the other hand, is represented by the right, which is the masculine and the left circuit, which is the feminine.

Owning our energy balls means starting to live our own lives, as opposed to stepping in line with someone else's. When we give in to other people, we're living their truth instead of our own. But when we own our energy balls, we own our truth and have the courage to live our own lives.

To own our energy balls means to support ourselves and our higher purpose. Owning our energy balls means having the courage to say "No," the courage to let go of friends, and the will to let go of behaviors and addictions on a physical level, as well as the ability to let go of old Pictures that no longer serve us.

We all hold onto things that aren't working. We stay in relationships far too long, or we stick with projects that are dead, desperately trying to make things work. Owning our energy balls means being able to connect and turn on our own flashlight, which means bringing awareness to our life and what it is we want to create and have. It means moving on the field and playing to our true Intentions.

Our energy balls represent our ability to ground the body. Grounding keeps us safe, secure, stable, and supported. It allows us to release what isn't working and make room for something new to come through. By owning our energy balls, we have power in the body to take action and to manifest our Intention.

Our energy balls remind us not to lose connection with the planet, the place where our batteries get recharged. We lose our grounding by not owning our energy balls.

Client Story

I have a client who, when we met, had gone through a bad divorce and lost everything. During the relationship, his wife had convinced him that he was mentally unstable and needed psychotropic medication. The relationship failed because of her pressure on him to constantly earn more money. Even though he was successful financially, she would demean his efforts and accuse him of being a poor provider and an inadequate parent. During the divorce, she convinced him to turn over all of his assets as compensation for his failure. He was controlled and beaten down by her aggression, even though all he'd ever wanted from their relationship was a happy home and family.

After the divorce, my client lost his job and drifted from one unsuccessful career attempt to another. His ex-wife continued to insert herself into his life and make self-centered demands that included controlling his relationship with their children. He continued to play into her Pictures and lost himself and his self-worth in the process.

When we began working, my first priority was for my client to take back his power and to begin building a new Foundation. He was fearful because he was intimidated by his ex-wife's chaotic and unstable energy. His problem, like that of many men, was that he was approaching her from a rational space. I had to teach him how to deal with her irrational energy and regain his power. Through a series of exercises, we worked on the creation of his Intention, as opposed to his current state of only responding to hers.

Within a month, working with me once a week, he began to regain his power. By the third month, he landed the best and most lucrative job of his career. He now remains calm with regard to his ex-wife, and her incessant demands have ceased in the face of his new energy. She had been like a live wire, seeking a place for her own energy to ground, and his constant acquiescence had made her feel unsafe, a situation that spun out of control. But his new ownership of his energy balls had created a Picture that she could play to, and the live wire that she had been all those years became grounded and secure.

We might attach to opposite types of people to try to create with or move our energy through someone. If so, we're subconsciously trying to balance and move our lives into Wholeness, but we're stuck on one side or the other.

ENERGYWORKS METHOD

1. ***Ground your energy balls.*** Start by holding two actual balls, one in each hand. They can be golf balls, tennis balls—any kind of ball—or you can order energy balls from me. Your right hand will be your masculine, or active, hand and represent your positive Pictures. The left hand is the feminine, or receptive, hand and represents creative chaos. For something to come into balance, you have to unify the two sides. For something to move, you have to complete two sides of the circuit. Hold your balls in the palm of your hands at the base of the spine. This method is to remind you not to lose your grounding. Ground to the center of the planet. Imagine a spiral drill that starts at the base of the spine and moves into the center of the planet to anchor you down. You can also imagine roots, like the roots of a tree. This is how you keep your body releasing in the present moment.

2. ***Activate the masculine side.*** This method is about setting your Intention and taking action toward your goal. Focus on the ball in your right hand. Put your Intention in the ball. Set the ball at a color that represents what you want. State your Intention aloud while looking at the ball. Create a clockwise circuit from your Heart to your right hand and back again. This will move you into action. Move like

the tide, out and back. Move to the Intention, pull back to the Heart, and feel the emotion of the goal. To create something, you must move your energy out, and you must bring your energy back. Focus on your Intention. Imagine that this ball in your hand rolls out in front of you and then back to the Heart.

3. ***Activate the feminine side.*** The feminine side is about receptivity and attraction of your Intention. Your goal is not to act. It is to be on the passive side and observe this space of what you want to release, transforming it into your Intention. Create a counterclockwise circuit from the ball in your left hand to your Heart and back. A negative thought may come in at this moment. By creating a circuit to your Heart, you are bringing the repressed aspect of stored energy back into relationship, simultaneously releasing it as fuel for creating your Intention. Don't have an opinion, criticism, or judgment of the feminine. Simply hold the space open and bring it back into relationship within the Heart. Just the awareness of it will provide fuel that powers you to receive and attract your Intention. What have you repressed? Depression is caused by the denial or suppression of true feelings. Allow yourself to feel your emotions. Stay with the feelings, even if doing so is uncomfortable for your feminine. Focus on your breath, and as you move your energy back to the ball, notice whether you have feelings of guilt or have been beating yourself up. Has your masculine side supported you? Bring these thoughts and feelings back to the Heart. Feel them, accept them, love them, and keep your Heart open. Bring the feminine

out of hiding and back into relationship. Stay with this movement until the pain disappears. You are reclaiming your power and your creative life force to manifest your goals in the world.

4. ***Create an Infinity Loop.*** Focus on the ball in your right hand to reset your Intention based on what you previously let go of. The way to take action is to open the Wisdom of the Heart to complete a circuit with your masculine side—the side of Intention, action, and moving your energy, step by step, to your goal. Instead of giving your Intention away to someone, pull your energy back to your Heart. Now, move your energy out and say, "I'm moving to my Intention, and I bring the Intention back to my Heart so I can have it." Focus on receiving your goal in the left hand. Imagine you are receiving what you asked for. Close your left hand around the ball that it's holding. Now, open your hand to receive your Intention and then close your hand and direct the Intention to your Heart so you can own it.

It is movement of our internal energy that creates a new reality in our lives. It enables us to own our energy balls and to own our space with energy that is unique to us. When we own our energy balls, we have the courage to let go of what we don't want, and we have the power to take action toward our goals. When we complete the circuit of the two sides, we achieve balance and activate the blueprint of our lives.

Journaling

Draw a line on a piece of paper. On the right side of the paper, draw a positive sign. On the left side of the paper, draw a negative sign. Then, on the right side, say one thing you want, and on the left side, say one thing you don't want. Now, draw a Diamond in the center and connect the Infinity Loops, connecting the two sides while focusing on being in the Diamond in the center. To create anything, you need to have the negative and positive overlap in the center.

Body Movement

Hold two balls, one in each hand, or imagine doing so. The right ball represents what you want. Move it to your Heart and around in a circuit to activate what you want. In your left hand, say what you don't want and move that in a circle to your Heart and around. (The direction does not matter.) Move your hand to the right (what I want) and to the left (what I don't want). One is the continuation of the other. Focus on having it in the space in between, in the Heart, which is the space where you create your dreams. Or, when you move into the Heart, you can also say, "I have it."

15

The Garden Within: Spirit in the Body

My parents went out on their first real date when I was four years old. They hadn't had two nickels to rub together in the period leading up to their marriage, and when the opportunity finally presented itself, they decided to have a night on the town. They hired the eighteen-year-old boy next door to babysit me, and that's when I was molested.

I remember the incident. I felt a strange energy take over me, but I was too young to know what to do. When I look back now, I have cleared the Pictures relating to the incident so that I am neutral to it. However, I still do recall the dark energy, like black tar, that I inhaled and that became trapped in my lungs.

My father found out what had happened, although I don't remember how. I remember hearing the boy next door being beaten with his father's belt and being sent away to the military. I also remember sitting on my father's lap and feeling his guilt that he wasn't able to protect me, along with his regret that he had chosen to go out that night with my mother.

There are many forms of molestation, and they involve not only a physical act but also an energetic one. Often, when certain friends of my father's were in our house, I had the feeling that they were looking at me sexually. Then, when I was in seventh grade, a neighborhood boy, five years older than me, became obsessed with me. I entered our garage one day without being seen and discovered him going through my laundry, smelling my clothes. My parents were generally away when I returned home from school, and this boy would somehow find his way into our house, where he would hold me down and molest me. His energy was similar to the boy who molested me when I was four years old, and like that other boy's parents, his parents were alcoholics. It was the same controlling energy coming into me, and no matter what I did, it would win. Years later, I realized that it was the pain inside these boys that entered into me and needed to be exhaled. Moving this through my Heart is what eventually transformed the black tar into light.

I didn't tell my parents, although I should have. Truth be told, I didn't even realize that I was being molested because the energy seemed to be coming at me constantly. I hated that boy, but he was my brother's friend. He was much older than us, and that put him in control. Both my parents had to work, so I would lock myself in the bathroom after school to stay safe. But in those days, I always seemed to be fighting off boys, and there was another boy in the neighborhood who came directly after me as well.

My father had a very generous heart and always helped those in need. He let people come into the house to stay with us, and I hated it. One young guy with addiction issues tried to force himself on me but was unsuccessful. My father found another fellow sleeping in the street and told him that he could camp in our yard. I could tell that the man was an alcoholic because he sent out a vibration that made me feel sick, a feeling that I had learned to recognize. It was that same controlling energy that sought to overtake me.

My father would often try to help these people by getting them construction jobs, but that would invariably lead to disaster. They would always fall back into their addictions, end up in jail, or even die by suicide. One man seemed to be getting his life together but ended up killing his ex-wife. But my dad was inherently a nice guy, and having been a foster kid accustomed to moving in and out of strangers' homes, he didn't perceive the constant presence of strangers to be unnatural. In retrospect, he probably felt the same way I did and was also being overtaken. It was just an energetic frequency that he got used to.

Many times, people are molested because the people closest to them allow it to happen. Growing up, I never seemed to think that being molested affected me. The last time it happened was when I was in ninth grade. My brother and I had a party at our house when my parents were away, and when I woke up the next morning, one of my brother's friends was having his way with me.

A part of me didn't think that I was molested because there was no real intercourse. It was *only* them putting their fingers in me and touching me, and I would become passive and paralyzed. More than anything, it was the dark energy that came in through this act that seemed to have an ongoing effect on me. It was about being overtaken, like being submerged in black tar. In these moments, my Spirit left me.

The frequency that resided in me from that initial molestation seemed to invite people into my life who wanted to overtake me emotionally as I grew older. Those people would boss me around or yell at me until I'd submit. I had a string of boyfriends who were extremely controlling, who monitored and wanted to attack me. Eventually, I realized that the incidents that affected me at a very young age had made me focus outwardly. I'd always focus on the people I was around, and never on myself. Since my own energy kept flowing outwardly, there was space for outside energy to overtake me in return, because when we abandon our space and are not filled up energetically, we leave ourselves vulnerable and open to be preyed upon. Countries get overtaken when they're divided. When we're divided individually, other people's energy flows in and controls our space. It's a form of molestation.

Whether we're overtaken at a young age or at any age, there's a part of our Spirit that leaves our body when this happens. If our energy leaves our body, that creates an opening for other energy to come in and overtake us. This behavior sets up an energetic pattern that will continue to play out on many different levels until we recognize it and call our Spirit's essence back.

After years of looking at other people's Pictures of being molested, I was finally able to see what actually happens on an energetic level. I've had many clients who have undergone years of therapy to clear their molestation. I can see that they've looked at the Pictures, but the perpetrator's energy still exists in them and they haven't been able to bring their own energy back. My own case was no different.

Years ago, I actually asked my husband if being molested could consist of being held down while somebody sticks their finger inside of you. I knew I was molested when I was four years old because of the aftermath, but I didn't have a concept of myself being molested in junior high school when boys forced themselves on me in that way.

When we don't possess our energy, our perception gets so distorted that we can't see accurately. In the case of molestation, the perpetrator's Pictures are distorting our innocence and trust. I have cleared the energy frequency of clients who have been molested, and it's like an entity in their space that doesn't want to leave. It continues to set them up in situations where they are controlled and overpowered on different levels. The takeover may not be in a physical way, but the subtler the energy is, the more sophisticated it can become.

Negative energy that enters you sets you up to kick you out of your space so that it can feed off you in the horizontal world. You know you're being overtaken because you feel paralyzed. Recently, I went over to my parents' house for a Father's Day barbecue, and as I was getting out of the car, I encountered a gentleman on the sidewalk who said, "I'm here to see your dad."

I said, "Who are you?"

He replied, "I just moved in down the street. I'm renting a room and he invited me over for the barbecue."

I said, "Wait a minute." I went into the house and saw my dad and I said, "Who is this guy? I don't like his energy."

My dad, as always, was just trying to be a nice neighbor. I said, "This is how people get molested. You bring it right into your house."

I knew that this was not a coincidence. It happened on Father's Day, and it reflected the lack of support and protection that I experienced growing up. I don't blame my father because he suffered the same wound from his own father. My father is a great dad, but when we carry energy with us, we continue to create the same energetic patterns. He told the man to leave.

I have two kids of my own, and I'm hyper-aware of the frequencies and the people they're around. One day my kids were running a lemonade stand with one of their friends outside our home. I was in my office in the back-yard and felt a wave of energy come back to me. It was the same frequency that I felt when I was overtaken in my youth. I went out to the front yard and asked my two kids and their friend what they would do if a gentleman came by in a van and asked for help to find his puppy. They didn't know how to respond, and I told them that they were to run away and start screaming. I said, "You're not allowed to help an adult without checking with me or your dad."

Later that same day, the boys went to a local baseball field and were sitting on some steps near the road when a man drove up in a van and asked for their help to find his lost puppy. The boys ran off screaming, as instructed, and told someone at the baseball facility. We found out that this man had earlier approached some other kids. There was an alert out, and the police were trying to find him. He was a kidnapper.

Many people have come to me with stories about molestation by someone they knew. What's interesting is that, in most of these cases, these people (the victims) are extremely intuitive. After a violation happens, those who have been violated approach the world like a surveillance camera, always watching. But unless those who have been violated clear the energy that came in on the violation, they will continue to be attacked and overtaken in different forms, either physically, verbally, or emotionally. This is how your energy gets hijacked. The attack happens to move your energy out of your space, and this sets you up to be overtaken.

When energy overtakes you, physical symptoms can be a side effect. Stomach issues, issues around the jaw and face—all kinds of physical ailments can come into play. You have this response because when your own energy leaves your space, you stop existing and your body responds. The way to protect yourself is to own your space and to fill yourself up with energy from the Unified Field and the planet.

Something within all of us drives us to find a sense of connection and a feeling of being whole, even if we don't always know that we're longing for these things. We look for this sense of connection to the external world in our careers, relationships, and families. We may have had a glimpse of it in a relationship where our Hearts opened for a moment. But later, our Hearts closed because the opposite happened: We became entangled, and we felt overtaken, controlled, stuck, and trapped. The relationship might die, even if we continue to stay in it.

When the external source of happiness disappears, so does this feeling of connection. The connection we once felt is replaced with disappointment and anxiety. This reaction puts us on the path of longing once again.

We may also try to solve our longing for connection in a career. Once we create the right career, we may have a moment of connection but soon begin to feel controlled and limited by the day-to-day demands of our occupation.

We long to create a family, thinking it will fill us, but many times the burden and responsibility of being in a family are overwhelming and we feel trapped. Then we long to have our own space and the freedom to have fun.

The mind tells us that what we are longing for is found externally, outside our own inner space, when the reality is that this sense of connection is found only in the Garden Within. Our minds can deceive us and show us Pictures that are mirages of what we want to believe but instead are unfulfilled promises that leave us empty and depressed. Once we begin to believe these Pictures, we are trapped. We don't know how to escape this view of reality and our energy stops moving.

When our energy is blocked, a serpent has entered our garden. We then find ourselves expelled. Our energy can't move because it only wants to find its way home, back to the garden. Soon we are wandering, lost in the desert, and we have forgotten who we are. Because we're disconnected, we have no energy to move or change or create. We feel imprisoned.

When we believe our minds in the same way that Eve believed the biblical serpent, we become controlling and try to micromanage people. We become obsessed with what is wrong and why things won't work. Our mind cuts off connection and communication with the body, and the effect is pain and anxiety. The body longs to be reunited with the Spirit, but as the serpent of judgment and criticism invades the garden, our circuits are disconnected by its presence, and all movement stops. Without the Spirit in the body, we are just containers, and when a container is empty, it will be filled with energy that is foreign to it.

In a desert, few things grow. Most people live in a spiritual desert. They believe the negative Pictures they're stuck in; this is the only reality they know. Their space is filled with chaos, doubt, and fear. When we're trapped in the desert, we try to connect to others to get the energy we need for survival. People hook into us, and we hook into them. When we live this lie, we lose our inner space; we become ungrounded, disconnected, and unconscious. Our relationships are about control and being superior or inferior. We either hijack someone else's energy, or they hijack ours.

The Spirit's true residence is the Garden Within. When we open our Hearts, we open the doorway for our Spirits to enter the garden. We are moving and flowing. We are connected to the Unified Field and are grounded to the Earth. To create anything, we must create it in the space of the garden; otherwise, it won't grow.

Four Signs That Your Energy Has Been Hijacked

1. Others take your energy because they don't have their own. They make you feel wrong and attempt to control you. These relationships are based on control and domination.

2. Others use your energy to create their own goals. They are able to do that because you think you're going to receive love and validation in return, but it never happens.

3. People you're close to create chaos and confusion, which disconnects you and allows them to overtake you. This disconnection divides your energy and, consequently, you don't know what to focus on. Without a focus, you're lost at sea and overtaken.

4. Your energy feels eclipsed: You move your attention out of your space, and it becomes filled with negative energy. Negative energy absorbs light like an eclipse and leaves you in the dark. If you can't see, you can't create.

The Heart creates an energy field around your space that is like a bubble. To find the Garden Within, you have to open to the Wisdom of the Heart and create your vibration in that space around you. What you have been longing for is found only in this garden, the place in your Heart where there is unity, peace, and tranquility. It is a place where you feel connected to everything and everyone, and where all things are whole. This is the space where you can experience your own true energy.

Client Story

A client I've known for about ten years literally grew up under the influence of a wicked stepmother. Before her father's remarriage, when my client was eight years old, she had been an intensely creative child. She had been connected to Nature, loved playing outside, and would make up stories for her friends when she was climbing and hanging out in trees. She was playful, joyful, and artistic. She was in relationship with her creativity and was living in the world in a natural way.

My client had a younger brother, and her new stepmother developed a habit of comparing my client to him, referring to her brother as cute and my client as ugly. The stepmother denigrated my client's storytelling and severely criticized her in ways that stifled her confidence and creativity. She also forbade my client from playing freely outside, claiming that it made her dirty, and this constraint cost my client her connection to the natural world. She retreated to watching TV and became isolated and filled with anxiety.

I began to work with my client when she was in her thirties. She had addiction issues, was unable to maintain a relationship, and was generally living in pain. My first step for her was to get back into relationship with the natural world as a way to get back into relationship with her true self. She took a meaningful job with an environmental company, and her life began to shift.

Since then, she has become happily married, has a beautiful young son, and is free of addiction and taking excellent care of her body. Her connection to her own child has rekindled her storytelling talent and her creative instincts in general. Her question now is, "What will I create?"

My client took a writing class at a local college and was asked to write about her childhood. The students took turns reading their work out loud, and my client's classmates responded in an overwhelmingly positive way to her work. We had a session shortly thereafter, and I encouraged her to start making up stories for her young son and taking him out into Nature. She began taking her son out into the trees and making up stories with him as the hero. She told him about his talent and courage, and through this process, her own excitement and creativity began to manifest physically.

My client reentered the writing class, imbued with the idea of telling stories to children, and with a whole new feeling of herself coming back to life and discovering the joy of playing in the garden. Surprisingly, her teacher lambasted her with a litany of every negative aspect of trying to publish books for children and thoroughly invalidated her goal. My client was devastated. She came home crying, convinced she would never write again. It was as if the serpent had invaded her Garden of Eden.

Fortunately, we had a session shortly thereafter. I told her that her writing teacher's criticism and discouragement were a reflection of her stepmother's cutting off her childhood creativity all those years ago. The putdown had stolen her creative energy and threatened to hijack her life. I brought her back on her timeline to her girlhood and the experience of having her creativity stifled. We invited her Spirit back into her garden and asked it to commit to creating with her body. In that moment, she remembered that, as a little girl, she used to call herself "The Queen of the Trees." This memory brought her energy back to her in present time, and she is now fully committed to working with children and creating children's books that establish a child's relationship with Nature. She plans to work with schools to teach children who are bullied and negated so that they can find the power they need to thrive within themselves. My client has a new commitment in her own life to her connection to her Spirit and body and to enjoying her own creativity in her own garden.

ENERGYWORKS METHOD

1. ***Call back your Spirit and commit to the body.*** Focus on opening to the Wisdom of your Heart. Move your energy inward through the doorway of your Heart to fill your garden. Ground your Heart to the planet. If there is a serpent in your garden, let it go. Connect to Spirit above and ask the Unified Field to fill your garden with light. Ask your Spirit's energy to return to you. Invite it back into the Garden. Invite it back into your body. Your body is the vessel in which the Spirit wants to reside, but when the body is filled with foreign energy, the Spirit can no longer enter. Your body is a temple. Open the door of your Heart and allow your Spirit

to come back. The Spirit likes to be free, to create, and it doesn't like to be limited by the mind. The mind can be critical in controlling the body. It's very important that you watch how the mind talks to the body, because if your attention is focused on what your body's not doing right, then the Heart closes and the Spirit cannot return.

2. ***Transform your trauma.*** When you have been abused, you become paralyzed and don't know what to do. As a result, people get stuck in the past and can't move forward. The Spirit's energy must return to that incident for you to be free. Identify a traumatic incident in your life and bring your awareness to it, which can set the stored energy free. Your attention may continue to recreate the incident in present time, or you may keep repeating it energetically. Go back on your timeline and see how the incident caused you to lose your connection, communication, and co-creation relationship between your Spirit and body. Ask your Spirit's energy to return to that moment. Observe the light filling that moment, so your Spirit can fill your body and move into present time.

3. ***Create a Body-Spirit connection.*** To truly create and manifest, we must connect the Spirit and the body. The body needs energy, and it needs the Spirit's attention. This makes it feel alive, youthful, and creative. Imagine that your Spirit is a kite that is connected to your Heart. Even if it wants to fly out to create and move, its energy can always come back to the Garden Within, filling you up with new energy and information. Imagine a circuit from the

Heart to the throat. The throat is located in the fifth chakra and is the expression of Spiritual creative energy. Let the energy move from your Heart, fill your throat, and move out through your arms and hands to activate your creative channels. Rub your hands together and touch different parts of your body, connecting to it and saying, "Hello, Body."

4. ***Create Body-Spirit communication.*** Ask your body what it wants. The more you can get into communication with the body, the more the body gets on board and creates with the Spirit. Even if the body doesn't answer, keep asking it what it wants. Does it want a walk? Does it want good food? Does it need to rest? Don't override what the body wants with what the mind is telling you. Remain in communication with the body, and your Spirit will come back into relationship with it. This is when manifestation happens.

5. ***Create a Body-Spirit agreement.*** The Heart brings the Spirit and body into relationship. Where they overlap in the Heart, the Garden Within creates the Greater Whole. One energy field connects to another energy field and creates a third field that is filled with the energy of the Spirit. Move the Spirit's energy from the Heart down to the lower belly, which is the second chakra. This is the energy center for physical manifestation. When you move the Spirit's energy in the belly, you access the center of your body's power. Imagine what you want to create and put it in your belly. Imagine that it is your baby and that you are connected to it and communicating with it. Ask for your body's agreement

with what the Spirit wants to create. The way to transform your life is to be in relationship with your Spirit. If you open to the Heart and find the Garden Within, the Spirit can guide and fill up the body. With this circuit of connection and communication complete, the Garden Within appears, and this is where things can grow without thought. The Spirit is playful, and the more it enjoys the body, the more alive it becomes. The Body-Spirit agreement is then on board, setting you free to create the magical life you really want to live.

Journaling

Write out your new agreement between what your Spirit wants and what your body wants and how they are going to work together. Have your Spirit and your body both sign the agreement so that they don't work against each other. Do this by asking your Spirit what it wants and write freely without thinking. Then ask your body what it wants and write, without judging, what the body wants. What the body typically wants is play time and leisure time or time to do something creative. Doing something creative is actually far more effective than doing hard work when it comes to creating your new life.

Body Movement

Walk your dog or imagine walking your dog where your Spirit is you and your body is the dog. Observe your Spirit leading your body. What is your Spirit kite? A dragon, bear, or colorful Diamond kite? When you are moving throughout the day, just look at the connection to your body. Are you criticizing your body? Are you really harsh in how you address the body? Start to have kind communication with your body. If you were Spirit, would you talk unkindly to your body? When our communication or connection is off and we become critical, we are looking for something outside ourselves to give us feedback. We are actually allowing an energy outside of us to determine who we are or a past energy or trauma to do so.

16

The Genie in the Bottle: Chaos to Creativity

People have said that I'm a Genie in a bottle and that I am their best-kept secret. In truth, I am an energetic facilitator or conduit between Spirit/God and Mother Earth. I've seen clients, one after the other, moving from joblessness to meaningful careers. I've worked with people who wanted a relationship and got one. What they've all sought in common was change on a deeply profound level, and I became a reflection of their unseen creativity. They first started seeing me because of some kind of pain in their lives, but ultimately, what they need is never really about what they first come in to see me about; instead, it's about them becoming Whole.

My job is to help people bring the unseen into manifestation. Even in the client's absence, I'm working on levels connected to their genetic line, or to their unconscious, or to the subtle levels of their dream space, or to their place in the collective unconscious. This is my female side in play. It consists of bringing creative life force into reality. My talent is to accurately see the Backspace (which is the unconscious) and to employ my female side to facilitate the emergence of light as the source of creation so that we can access it and use it to create my clients' goals.

When my clients have had experiences that cause their personal Genie to be closeted, I enter their space and release their creative energy, letting the Genie out. From there, they are able to move forward in the world without concern about judgment or criticism. They own their creative energy outright.

In my work, I'm continually faced with people accustomed to not supporting or validating these creative attributes. As a healer or giver, I may actually appear weak to others because I support them unconditionally, but I know this opinion of me isn't personal. It's merely a reflection of how the Genie has generally been hidden and suppressed in our culture.

We find ourselves doing what other people ask because we're trying to maintain harmony and to create balance without being true to our creativity. I've known many people who've had horrible divorces from partners who lambasted them as inadequate during their time together, just to keep them giving. They continued to suffer and to do what was asked because they didn't stand up and say, "Enough." The greatest freedom any of us can achieve, male or female, is the refusal to be in agreement with pain and to step away from any relationship where we're consistently held at fault.

The Genie in the bottle is a good analogy for how we all hide our creative energy and how we often don't support the person who is bringing energy to our projects, our life, or our ideas. It's often hard to stand up and ask for what we need and what we deserve, but if we fall back on acceptance and allow the Genie to remain hidden, then we remain hidden as well.

Many people believe that creation happens through action, but the source of creation is passive. The Genie in the bottle is the unconscious creative force. In balance, there is wholeness, for men and women both. From wholeness comes the fulfillment of our wants and needs, and everyone wins in the end.

The conscious part of you limits the creative force within you because it wants to control you. The passive side wants to have fun effortlessly creating, but the mind puts that down, constantly invalidating your freedom of expression by censoring and judging. This belief that you need to impress to be able to create is planted in you from the time you're young. If you feel that you're not good at something or that the thing you create isn't perfect, you won't even try to create it in the world.

Negative thoughts and feelings that you manifest get stuck in your body, preventing your body and energy from moving, and if you can't move, you can't create. When your mind projects its doubts and anxieties, the body reacts by not wanting to be in communication. This creative process is really about embracing the pain in the body (which the mind has afflicted us with) and turning it into creative expression.

The more you get into communication with the unconscious creative force, the more it will create for you. The more you don't let the mind control your creative force, the more creations will magically appear. When you repress your emotions, deny your thoughts, or reject the body, the Genie will get your attention by continuing to create the opposite of what you want. But when you let the Genie out of the bottle, you're letting negativity out of the body and letting go of the conversation that your mind has engaged in with the negative. Most people don't want to be negative, but what shows up in the external world is a reflection of how you create in the internal.

Expressing your creativity is a process of healing. The end result is never the issue. The release of creative energy is tied to the very fabric of your being and is a key component to your overall health and peace of mind.

Client Story

My client Jill works for an advertising agency. She came to me because she always experienced severe anxiety when presenting her ideas at work. She had a deathly fear of not being perceived as competent. Her creativity was stifled by her concern about what people might think of her when they heard what she had to say. The result was that her creativity retreated and closeted itself, much like the Genie in the bottle.

Jill's mother was a naturally creative person who shut down her own source of expression when she began to have children, as a way of conforming to the notion her generation embraced that motherhood and creative enterprise were incompatible. I looked at Jill's own timeline, and she couldn't recall a period of her life when she felt at ease expressing herself. Although she couldn't point to a single incident as a beginning to this, it entailed four different elements. First, her mind was critiquing everything she tried to create, as she was creating it. Next was her negative perception of what other people thought of her ideas. Third was the assumption that her creations had to be perfect to be valid but never could be. Finally, there was the fear of exposing her creation to the world. All of this led to her Genie being trapped within.

Jill also began to see this process play out in her kindergarten-aged daughter. She once observed her daughter showing a paper lantern she'd made in school to a male classmate. The boy took the lantern out of her daughter's hands, declared that it was ugly, and tore it. Jill stood by watching this interaction and, after they left school, saw her daughter break down completely, having bought into her classmate's criticism and cruel rejection of her creative effort. Experiencing this situation brought Jill's own history of stifled creativity blatantly back to life, as she recalled a similar incident in her own childhood. She didn't know what to say to her daughter other than to commiserate because the incident validated her own negative feelings about the inevitable rejection of creative expression.

Not long after the incident with the lantern, Jill's daughter told her that she wanted to dance in the school talent show. Jill already had formed an opinion of her daughter as a poor dancer, and she was so afraid of her daughter giving a bad performance that she informed her husband she wouldn't attend the show. Jill was scared beyond reason that other people would condemn her daughter's performance and that her daughter would in every way be worse off for having put herself forward.

What Jill and I worked on was based on her daughter's lantern. Her daughter's name is Lucia, which means *light*. We visualized a creative lantern of light, located within, that no one can take away and that no one can judge. We agreed to shine this inner lantern out into the world, embracing the creative light and owning it. We had Jill support her daughter's performance in the talent show as a way of supporting herself. Jill had been focused on her daughter's shortcomings as a reflection of her own, and she now restored her own self-worth by focusing on the expression of her daughter's creative light and the fact that her daughter could own it.

Furthermore, the energy that Jill had expended upbraiding her daughter was now harnessed into creation. After only two of our sessions, she made a presentation at work that resulted in unprecedented praise from her bosses. This response lit Jill up and left no room inside of her for self-doubt or second thoughts. It put her in the moment and allowed her to create spontaneously. She has discovered the bliss of unrestrained expression, and now she's sharing that with her daughter. Her inner Genie has found its path to the outer world.

ENERGYWORKS METHOD

1. ***Say "Hello" to the Genie.*** To unleash the Genie within, you must say "Hello" to the passive creative force. Nod your head in agreement with the Genie's creation, give it permission, and thank the creative force for its gift. You must support how it creates, saying, "And so it is." You may feel chaotic because the passive side feels out of control, but you must trust the passive side's ability to create and be just a little patient. It's like a baby that you can't see until it comes into the physical world.

2. ***Embrace what you don't want in the inner world.*** Place your left hand on your stomach while identifying what you don't want. Feel the energy, like fear or doubt, that keeps you from moving and that consequently stops you from creating. Embrace this energy and move it by moving your hand counterclockwise in a circuit from your stomach to your Heart. Use the energy of what you don't want as a force with which to create.

3. ***Identify what you want in the outer world.*** Place your right hand on your stomach and feel the positive energy, like courage, passion, or self-expression, that this brings up. Move your hand clockwise in a circuit from your stomach to your Heart, and in doing so, move the energy, express it, and use it to create with.

4. ***Identify the space in between.*** See what emerges from the space between what we want and what we don't want. These elements are like bookends that define the boundaries of creative space. In this process you're activating both the inner and outer worlds, and the space in between is where creation can occur. This is the unknown space that sets up new possibilities and pure creativity. Let it unfold.

5. ***Thank the Genie.*** When you communicate and bring the Genie back into relationship in the Heart, you will create as one and have fun co-creating. Acknowledge your connection to the creative unconscious, and find joy in the ways that your creation can be reflected in the greater world. The more you validate the unconscious creative force, the more it can be released from its bottle and can express itself in the world. If you release the Genie within, your world will reflect oneness. The mind will try to hang on to what you don't want and use it to discourage you and stop you from shining your eternal light into the world. But if you embrace what you want, along with what you don't want, and put these two opposites in motion, the Diamond space that shows up in between will be the field that you can play and create in. It's the magical space of simply being.

Journaling

Unleash the Genie by asking it to create something and see what shows up. Give the Genie full permission to create. You are basically asking the Genie to create the unknown and seeing what shows up. Don't have any expectations or opinions or judgments about what you want or don't want. Give the Genie full permission to create from the unknown.

Body Movement

Hold a ring or keychain or draw a circle in the air with your finger and look at the empty space in between. Imagine an empty space. Say, "I focus on the space in between to create my dreams." The empty space in between is the magic to create your dreams.

Conclusion: From Coal to Diamonds

Diamonds are arrayed in interlocking tetrahedral pyramids of carbon atoms. Tissues in our body are also aligned in structured, repeating patterns like in a Diamond. The molecules of our muscles, bones, eyes, cell membranes, collagen, elastin, even our DNA, all have crystal-like structures. Our bodies can be considered as liquid crystals, and even small movements create electric fields and currents.

—Energy Medicine in Therapeutics and Human Performance by James Oshman

It is important to connect to the light of Spirit, to the star energy of the sun, and bring its light into the physical body—to the inner core, which is our Heart. Then the light within us will eradicate the dense, dark energy in our lives. Even if things are falling apart in our world and the world around us, running this light will allow us to experience peace, freedom, and joy. We will be able to walk with certainty in any situation. Our inner light is our power.

In other words, we all have an inner crystalline structure, and in a very real way, when we move our inner energy and open up to the Wisdom of the Heart, Diamonds are made. When we focus on the light within us, we begin to activate our Diamond body, refracting and reflecting light outward, causing us to shine. When our energy emanates out from our Hearts, we can't be overtaken. When we focus on the Diamond of the Heart, we activate our very nature, the star energy within us.

We are made of the stars, and when we remember who we are, our own star burns bright. Our communication becomes one of light, where our Pictures are projected, reflected, and refracted through the network of the Unified Field. We are the conduits through which the network is connected from above and below.

As I resisted myself through the years, my family and the other people in my world also resisted. But as I shifted, they shifted with me. My greatest success story is myself and those people to whom I'm the closest. My mom and dad are happy and financially secure, living in a remodeled house. My brother overcame a life-threatening illness of his own, has a great job, and has a wonderful wife and a son who will be that family's first college graduate. My husband is coaching youth and has a successful career, and we have two beautiful sons of our own. My practice is thriving and so are my clients. We all still confront the negative, but we use its chaos as fuel for creativity.

The very Foundation on which I was born is depicted by my maiden name, Carbone, which means *coal* in Italian. Coal originates from dead plant and animal matter and is used as fuel. It is mainly composed of carbon, which is the building block of all living matter. Then, when I got married, my name changed from coal, Carbone, to Bellisimo, the most beautiful. That's actually my husband's name, and to me it has always signified Diamonds.

Diamonds are crystals that have been transformed from raw carbon over three billion years, and in the same way, all of our Foundations are carbon that can be transformed into Diamonds. Some of us may have gotten an easier start than others, but each of us has been born onto our own playground, and each of us has different things we need to transform so that we can evolve and grow. By learning how to transform our personal playground through moving from the negative to the positive to the Greater Whole to the Space in Between (the Unknown), we can transform the larger playground that we all share: the playground of Mother Earth.

Chaos is the coal that fuels my creativity. Being overtaken by the chaos from relationships, financial issues, and careers showed me where my energy got stored and where it was stuck. This book has been a story about how we all get overtaken in the game of life and how we can turn that around and create. I've described a life to you with family issues, with physical issues, and with learning disability issues—with issues of being overtaken by objects and by people. There are Pictures of being overtaken by poverty through a financially deprived upbringing, sexually by boys and men, intellectually by learning disabilities, emotionally by attacking and controlling relationships, and generally by the self-doubt and low self-esteem that resulted from all of these Pictures. But it's a story, above all, about how I found my way out by finding my way in. It's a story about opening to the Wisdom of the Heart.

Consider the peacock in the dump. The peacock observes its surroundings to find food. It chooses to eat poisonous plants and snakes and then transforms the poison into its beautiful plumes. Choose to observe your life like the peacock. Eat your fears and use them to nourish your Heart to transform them into light. Eat your poisonous thoughts and feelings and release what you don't want. Let that fuel your Intentions. Turn your coal into Diamonds.

Let the new game begin. This is the journey within.

Glossary

Backspace: The dark closet in our subconscious where thoughts, feelings, and emotions get stored. When we are not in relationship with it, it drives us.

Greater Whole: The place in the Heart where the Backspace and Intention Space overlap to create something greater than the sum of the parts.

Heart: The space where all spontaneous creation happens and the unknown comes through.

Infinity Loop: The heart creates in a circle and unifies all things in a never-ending loop of the creation process. The opposing sides of the Infinity Loop create the Greater Whole.

Intention Space: The conscious space of what we want to create.

Pictures: Mental images connected to thoughts and emotions.

Unified Field: The dynamic connectivity of everything.

Wisdom of the Heart: The place where original creation happens.

Author Biography

Kim Bellisimo, MA, is not your typical life coach, counselor, or energy worker—although she is all three. Highly intuitive from a very young age, Kim knew an embarrassing amount of personal information about the people around her. But she didn't know what to do with it.

As an adult, Kim found her abilities growing stronger, and she became a sponge for people, often absorbing their physical and emotional pain. This ability led to many of her own health problems, including chronic fatigue syndrome, fibromyalgia, thyroid issues, and joint pain. In her twenties, she realized that she had to learn tools to clear this negative energy and create new, healthier patterns of engaging with others.

Motivated by a desire to heal her body, Kim set out on a journey to discover and develop tools to help her along her own transformative path, which led to the development of her EnergyWorks modality, a Heart-based system for creating new possibilities. She earned a master's degree in Life Transition Counseling from the University of San Francisco, which provided her with a psychological framework within which she uses the intuitive skills she was born with. Working with thousands of clients and groups around the world, she has witnessed how her tools can work for anyone who wants to leave behind old habits and hurts and create the freedom, joy, and love that they deserve. She has discovered that it is possible to change impossible situations and to create unimagined new realities.

Kim lives with her husband and two sons in northern California, where she has a thriving private practice and conducts the same workshops and training that she teaches around the world. She offers both in-person and virtual private client sessions, group classes, and workshops. *From Chaos to Creativity* is her first book.

Acknowledgments

The reason this book exists is that I had Richard Gelernter, an amazing artist and Renaissance man, to write down the first version of my story. I also want to thank my good friend, Jill Sobolewski, for editing my story. I want to thank Jan Johnson Drantell, who guided my book to publication. I especially want to thank my clients who have donated money to support my book: Nancy Kukacka, Sobia Shaikh, Clare Kavanagh, Kirsten Senbruch, Noe Chavez, Rachael Delamontana, Melanie Lamoureux, Ariele Andrakin, Stacie Solt, Susie Arnett, and many more. Finally, I want to thank my loving family, Tony, Dwight, and Matteo Bellisimo, and my parents, Dwight and Joyce Carbone, without whom my journey to transformation would not exist. I love you all. In Greater Whole.